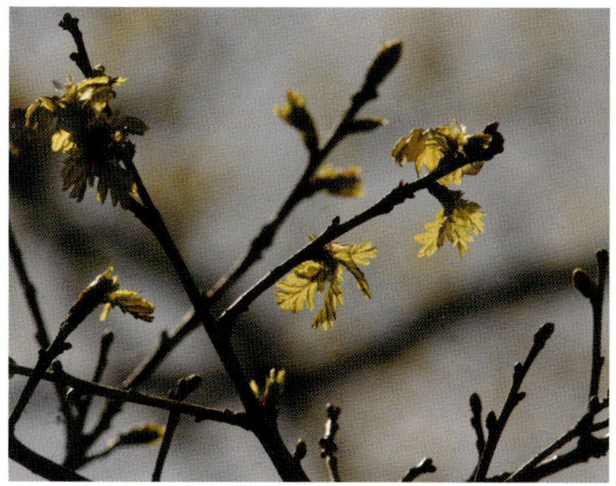

CHRIS MORRIS took up photography after dropping out of university. After three decades of corporate photography, he moved to Gloucestershire and reverted to documentary work, linking it to his long interest in industrial history. He has held several exhibitions of his work and published a number of books on landscape and industrial heritage *(see back cover)*.

First published 2007 by Tanners Yard Press

Tanners Yard Press Church Road Longhope GL17 OLA
www.tannersyardpress.co.uk

Text and images © Chris Morris 2007

British Library Cataloguing in Publication Data
A catalogue record for this book is available from the British Library

ISBN 09542096-7-2
ISBN 978-0-9542096-7-4

Designed by Paul Manning
Printed and bound by Alden
De Havilland Way
Witney
OX29 OYG

Dean's Big Oaks

AND OTHER SPECIES

Chris Morris

Foreword by Rob Guest

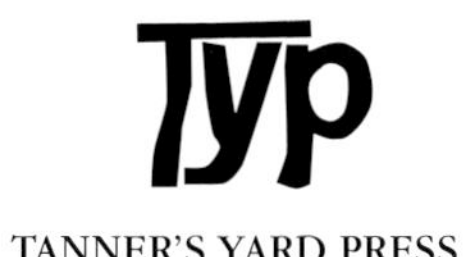

TANNER'S YARD PRESS

PREFACE

Having published two photographic books on the Forest of Dean, one revealing the remnants of the old industries and the other a celebration of the area's landscapes, traditions and cultural diversity, I felt it was appropriate to pay attention to an aspect I had not previously addressed: the woods themselves.

This is not a technical book on trees, nor a comprehensive catalogue, but I hope it is more than a random sweep across the woods and hedgerows. It begins with the big oaks which are associated with Dean's history, many of them named after past Deputy Surveyors or for other reasons. It goes on to explore a wide range of other interesting specimens, and finally looks at the wood workers who plan, manage and use the timber.

Most of the photographs were taken on land with public access. Some were taken on private property, and readers wishing to see particular trees or settings for themselves are asked to respect this. Grid references are supplied where appropriate and some directions are given. Both appear in bold type. Other sites may be located from the map on page 72 or from the Sculpture Trail map available from the Forest visitor centre at Beechenhurst Lodge.

Chris Morris

Contents

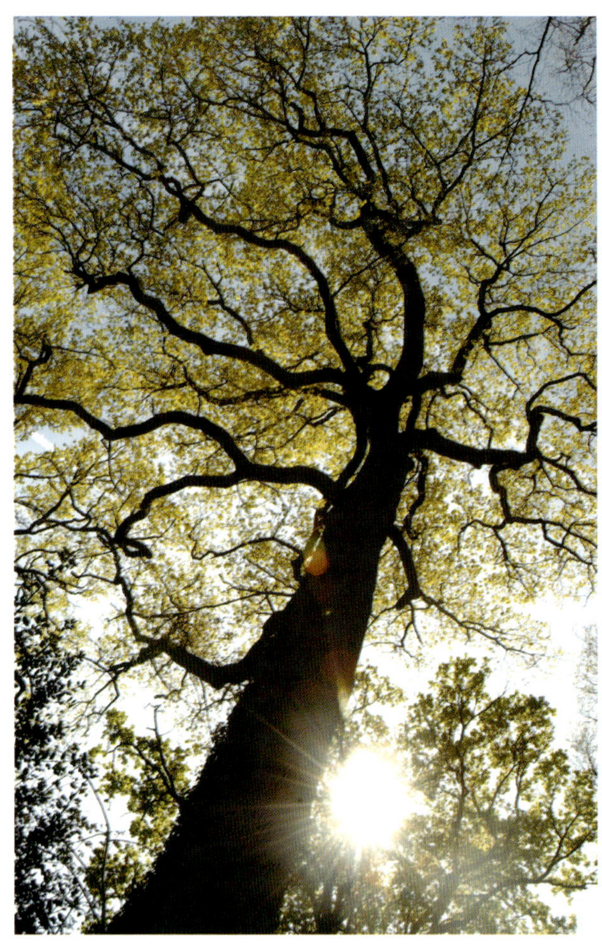

SANZEN-BAKER

A typical forest oak, its tall straight trunk forced up towards the light under competition from adjacent trees. Sanzen-Baker was Deputy Surveyor from 1954–68 and is credited with opening up the Forest for public use.

617119 Close to 'Melissa's Swing' on the Beechenhurst Sculpture Trail (see page 80)

FOREWORD

As Deputy Surveyor for the Dean, I have a professional interest in trees based on a deep love of their beauty and an appreciation of the many benefits they bring – in the landscape, as homes for wildlife, as sources of timber, or simply for shade or shelter. Forests are places of trees: one would assume that our ancient forest would have many ancient trees. In fact the history of exploitation described in the first chapter of this book means that, with the exception of churchyard yews, the Dean's oldest trees date from the mid-seventeenth century. Despite this there are still many big, even champion, trees and others noteworthy or interesting for a variety of reasons.

The Dean is most famed for its oaks and these rightly take pride of place in this book. Chris has searched for and recorded many of the named trees, as well as other noteworthy specimens, and trees other than oak are also given due attention.

This collection of photographs should inspire people to look at the woods of the Dean with fresh eyes. I hope that it will encourage many to follow Chris's example and search out specimens of particular interest and that it will help foster a greater appreciation of the value of the trees in this wonderful forest.

Rob Guest
October 2007

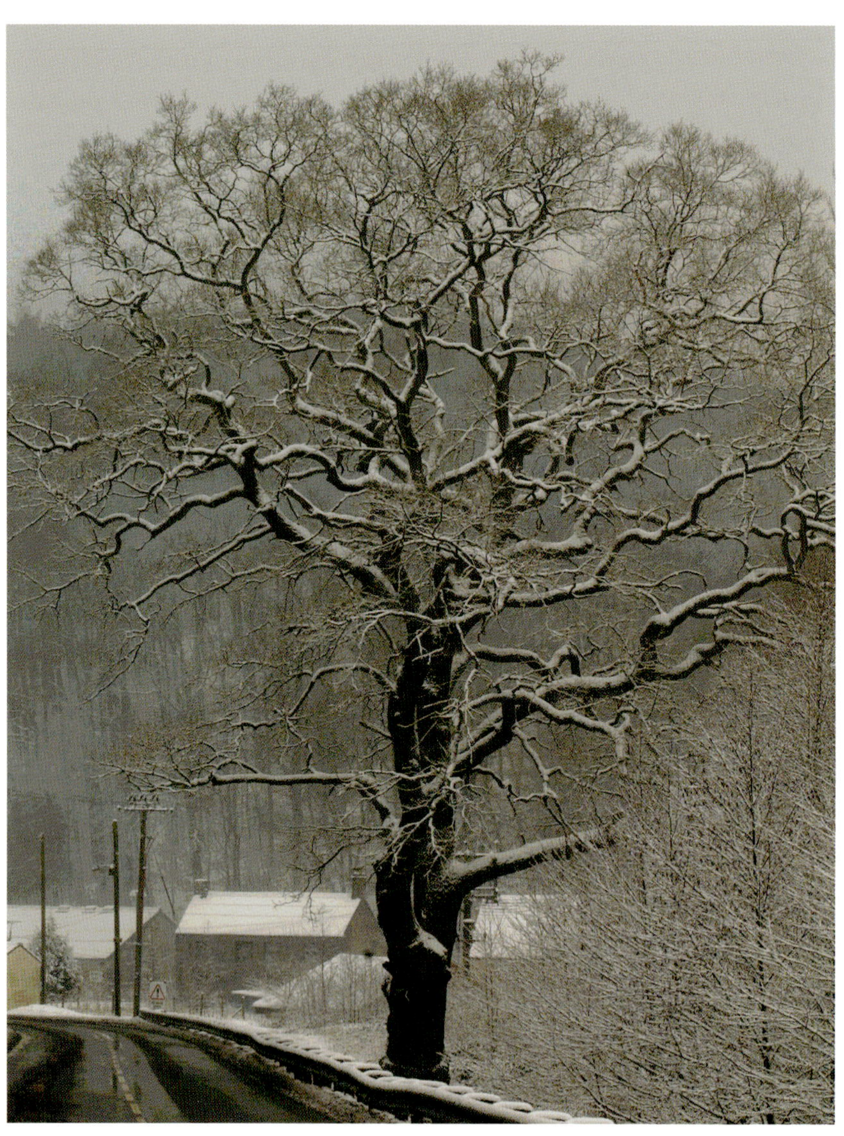

1
BIG OAKS

When the Romans first arrived in Britain, the area we know as the Forest of Dean, wedged between the confluence of the rivers Wye and Severn, already had a reputation for the production of iron and other minerals. Indeed, it is one of the reasons the invaders came. Success in iron smelting depended on the supply of charcoal from the area's extensive oak woods.

A millennium later, William the Conquerer took the Forest as one of his personal hunting grounds. This did not put an end to charcoal production, but it did lead to the area acquiring a distinctive and lasting character. Like other hunting grounds such as the New Forest, Dean was subject not to the country's gradually evolving common law but to a Forest Law. Legacies include the old rights of grazing and pannage, and the historic title for today's head of the Forestry Commission in Dean, that of Deputy Surveyor, was created in 1633.

By the end of the sixteenth century the natural regeneration of the oak woods, which was possible with only small-scale felling, was under pressure. As well as being used as a local construction material, Forest timber was increasingly in demand for shipbuilding for the navy. By the middle of the seventeenth century the shortage of mature oaks was seen as a major problem. In 1668, Charles II's government enacted legislation severely limiting their use for charcoal. Oaks were to be seen as a resource to be conserved, and felling was accompanied by replanting. Enclosures were instituted to prevent damage caused to young trees from grazing.

This regime suited the navy, but it was bad news for the iron producers; indeed, it drove the developing industry up the Severn to Coalbrookdale. By the time coke furnaces were introduced, Dean had lost its position as the country's main centre for the production of iron. However, for the sake of the woodlands, we should be grateful, as many of today's big trees owe their survival to the 1668 Act.

VERDERERS' OAK

Verderers, and their court, tried to balance the interest of the King and the demands for timber. This oak dates from the mid-seventeenth century. With its rather small crown, it was probably pollarded early in its life, the branches possibly being taken for charcoal burning.

There are very large oaks near Littledean but this is the 'stoutest' in the statutory Forest – over 23 feet round, a measure confirmed by Ben Lennon of the Forestry Commission. (See also page 72.)

619119: Close to the Speech House (where Verderers still hold court), opposite the cottages on the New Fancy road.

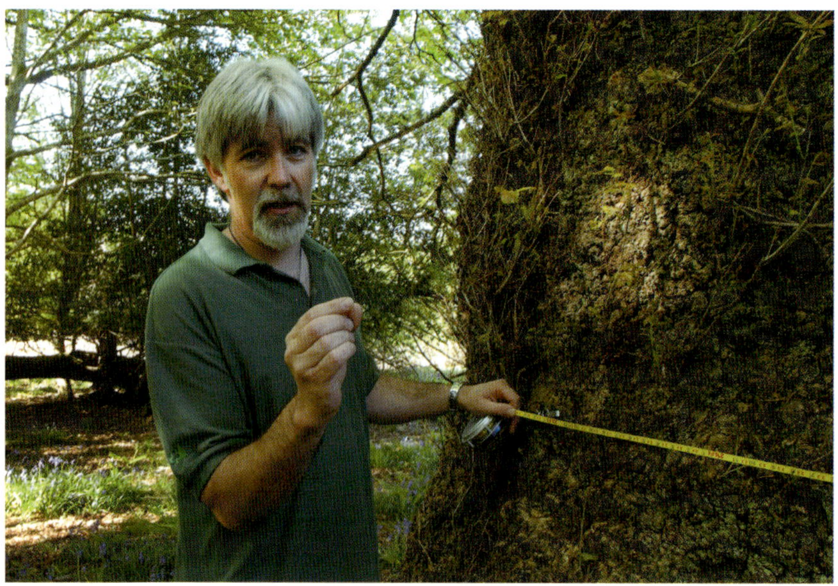

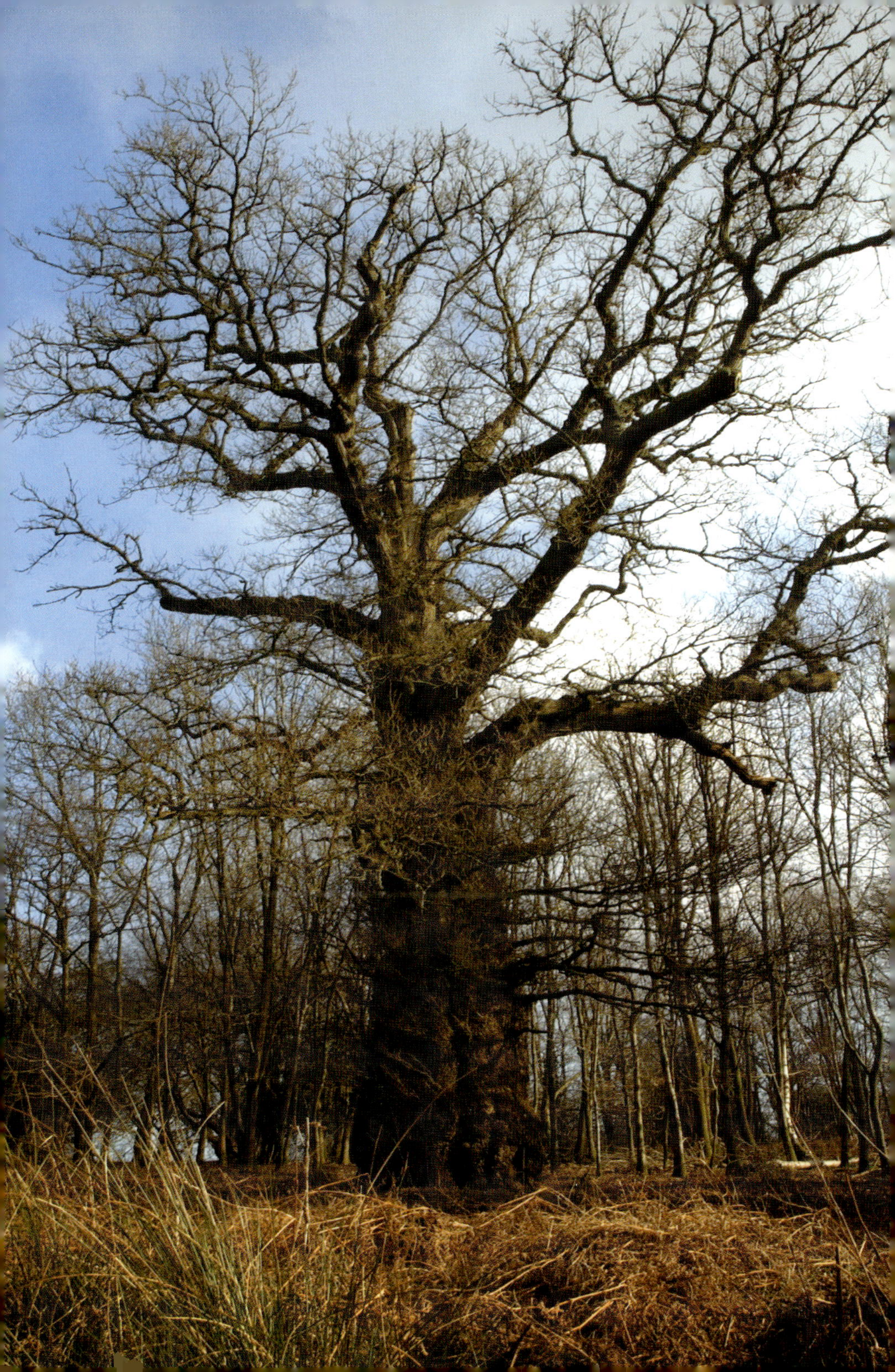

Charles II Oak

Year 6 children from Parkend Primary School measure the girth of Charles II oak with their outstretched arms. Allowing for holding hands and a bit of slack, it comes to just under 23 feet – about seven metres. (See also page 90.)

625088: See map on page 72.

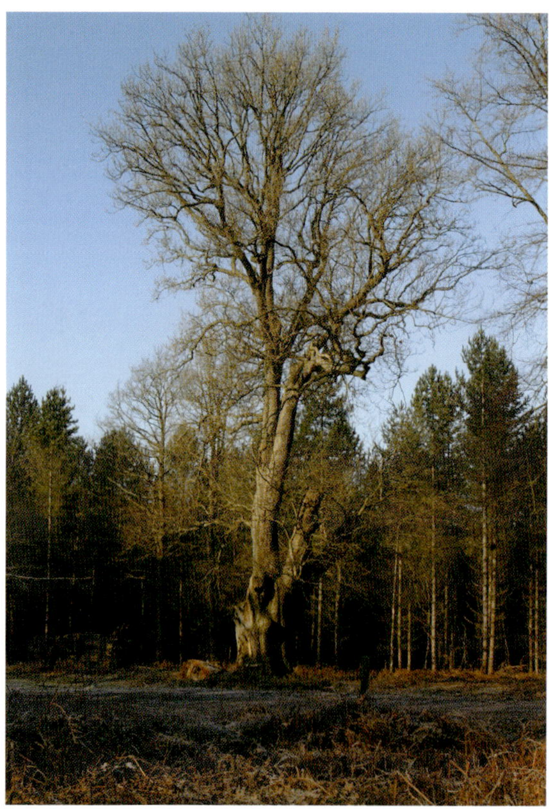

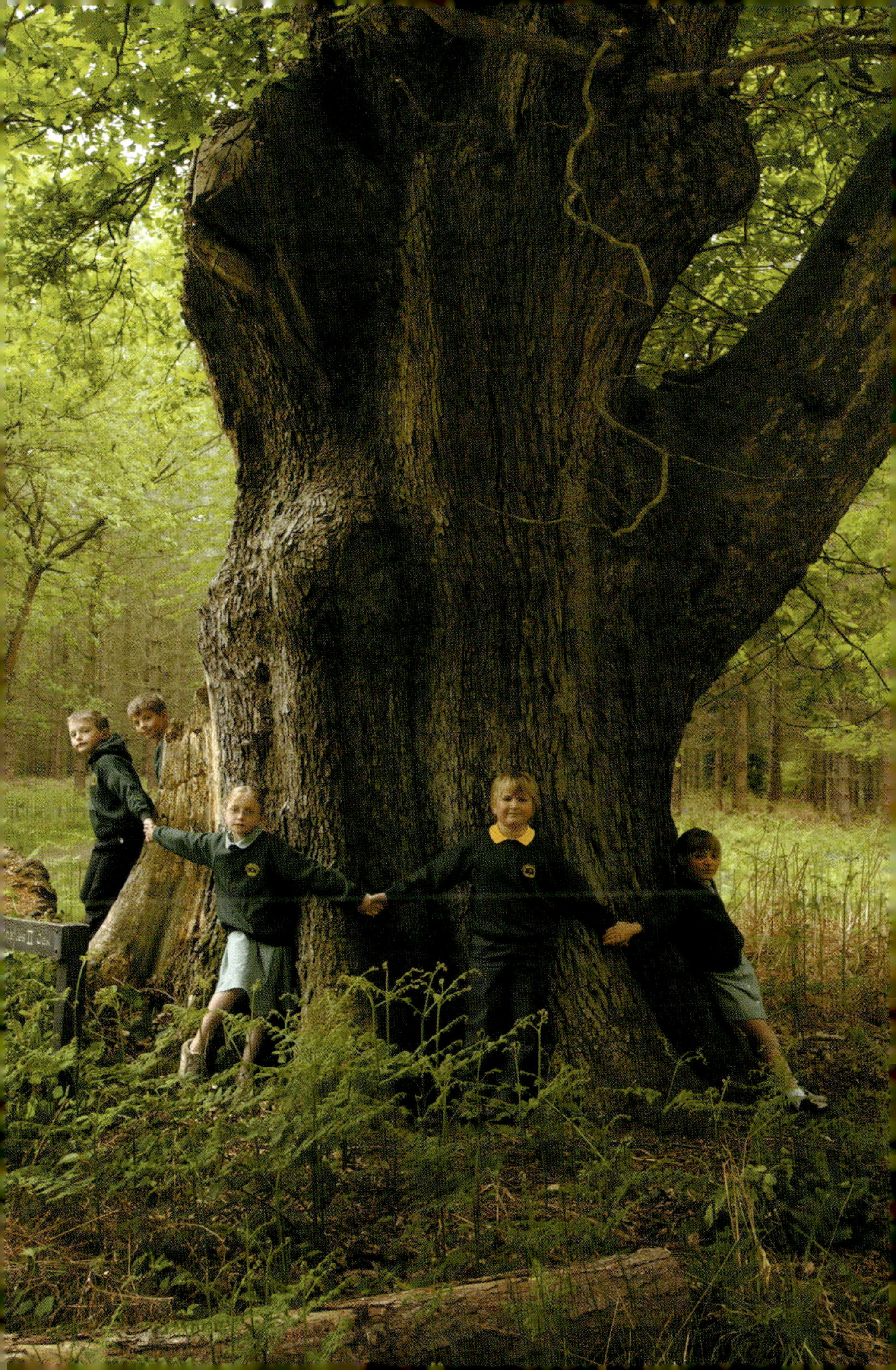

Forest Giant

Another huge seventeenth-century oak, standing in its own clearing, but screened all around by coniferous woods

626085: See map on page 72.

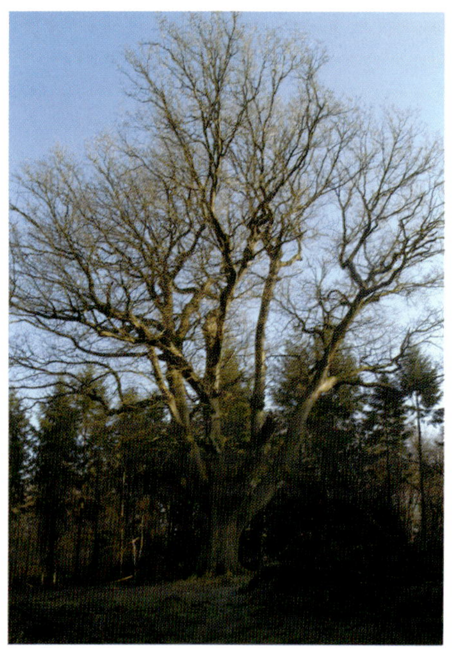

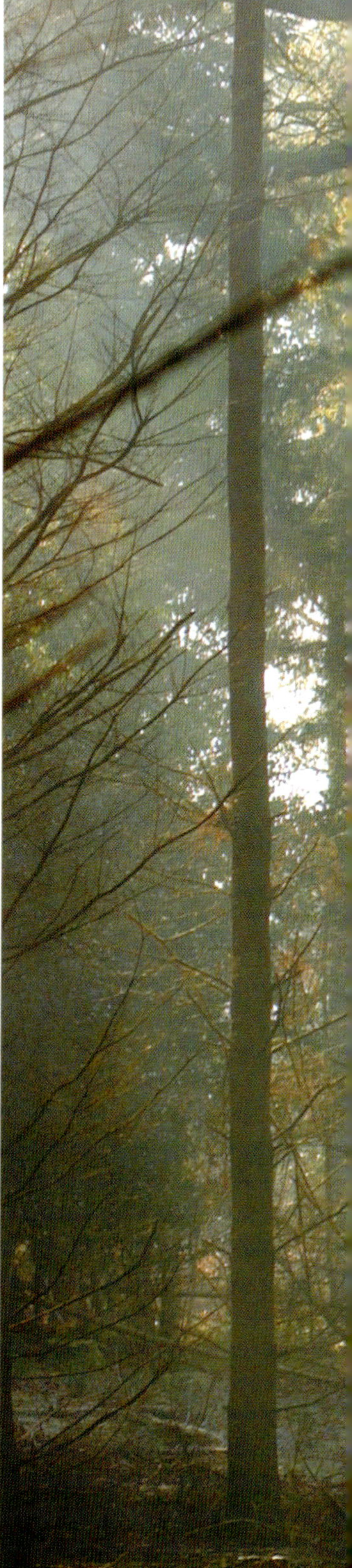

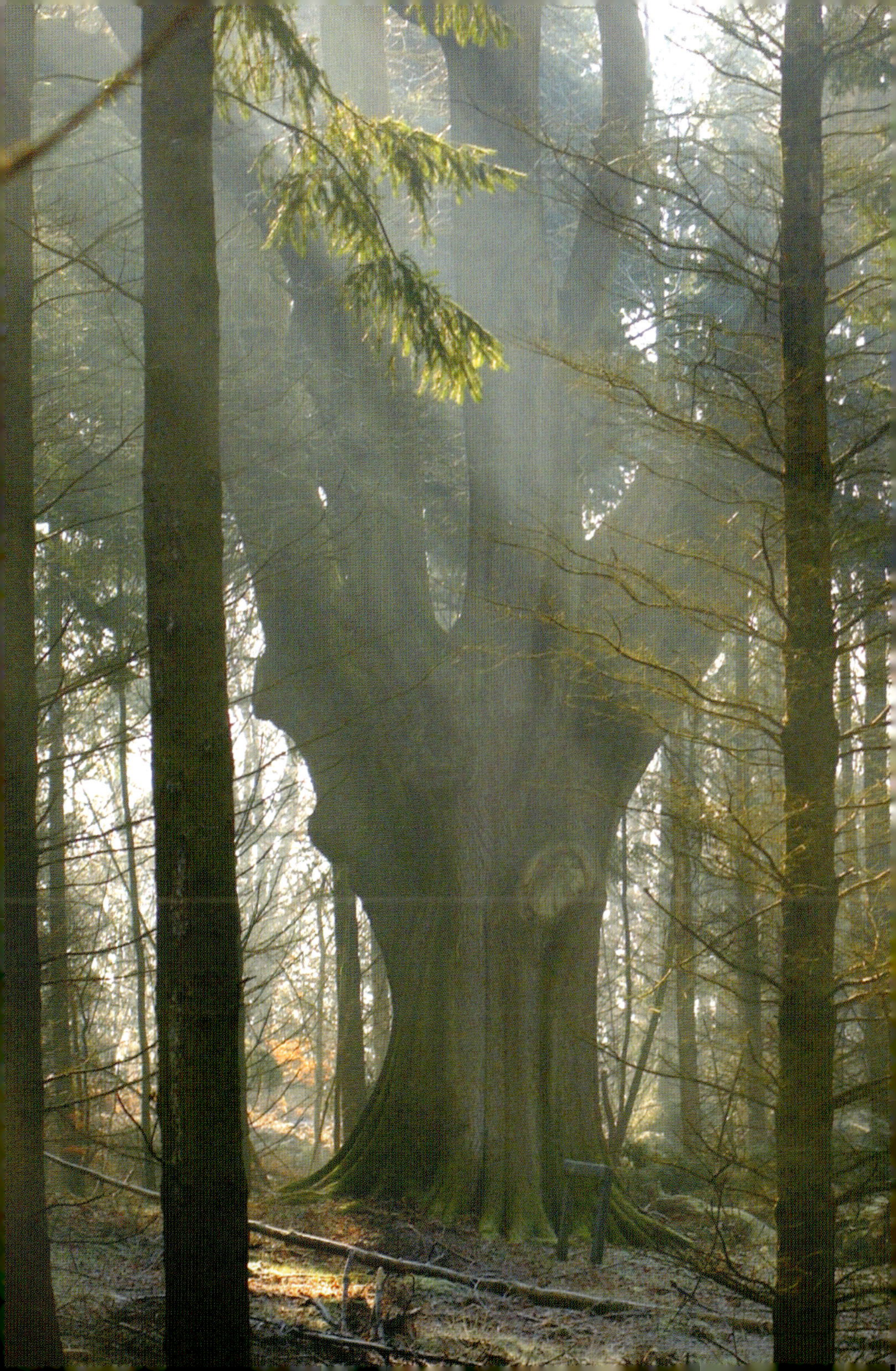

SHADEN TUFT

This oak is in the same section of woods as Forest Giant and Charles II, and is the same age. The four-way split trunk could be a result of pollarding at a young age (see page 10).

Below: This fine shaped oak on the cycle track near New Fancy probably grew from a hedgerow.

630092 (opposite), 627094 (below). See map on page 72.

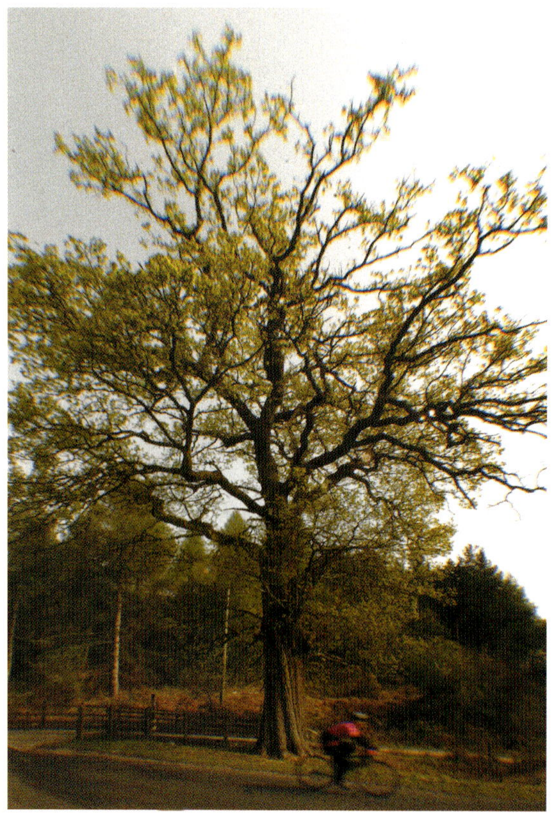

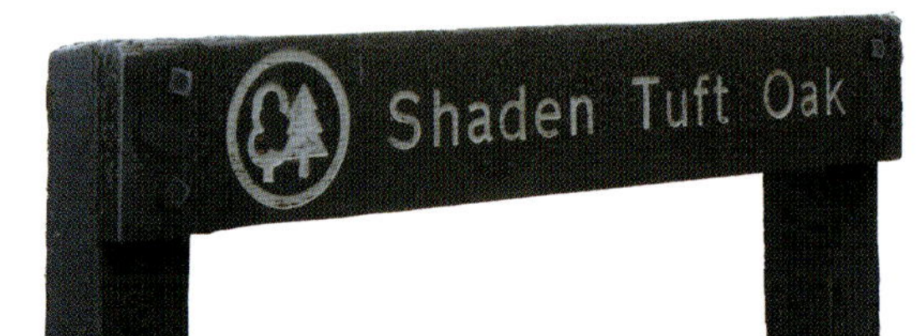

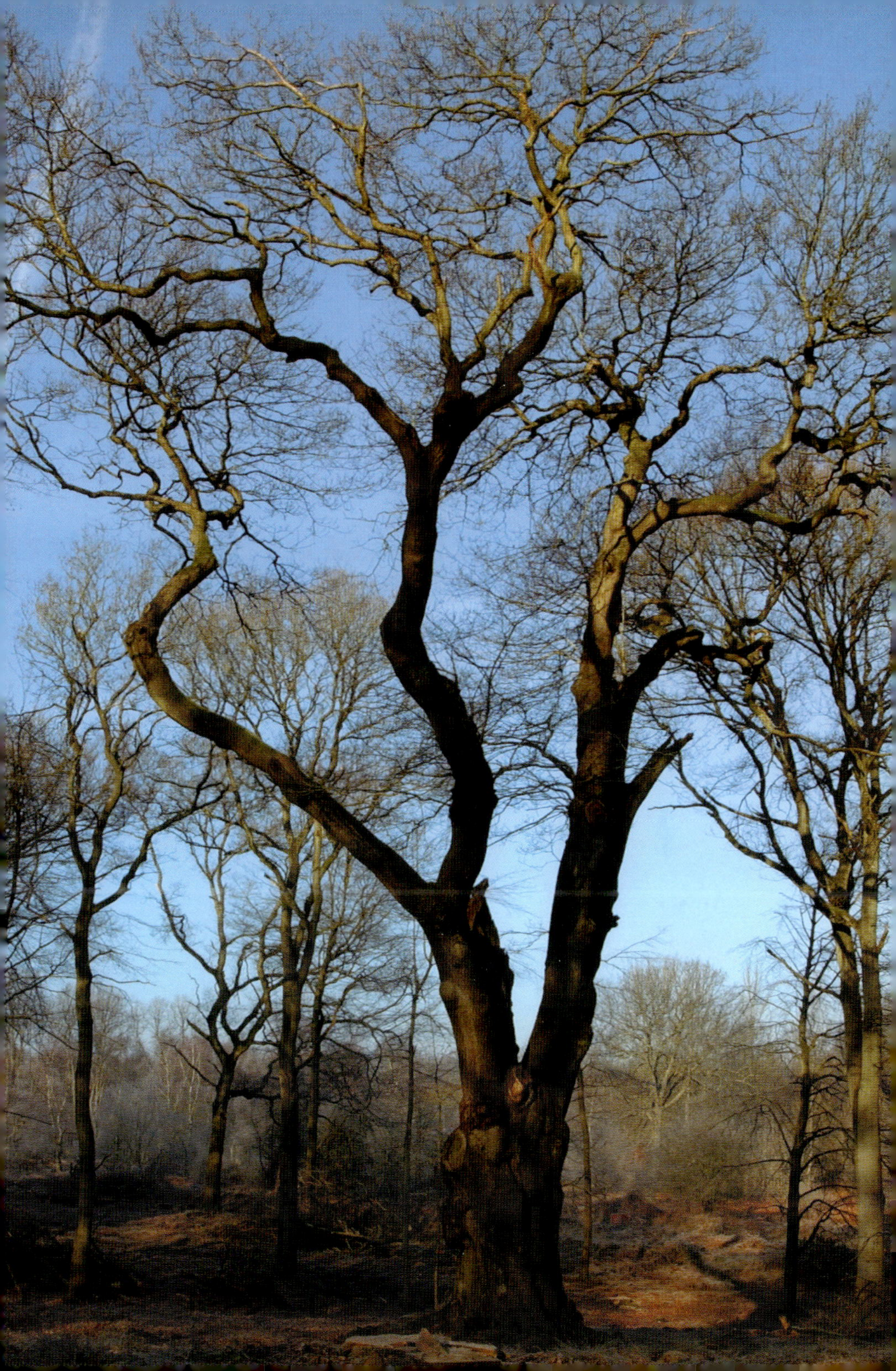

BURDEN OAK

The 300-year-old Burden Oak, reputed to be the heaviest in Dean (about 18 tons), rises majestically above a clearing prettily decorated in May with wild garlic.

The tree was named after the Rev. John Burden, Rector of English Bicknor in 1844. When the rest of the wood was felled in the 1950s, it was saved by the then incumbent, Rev. Walker, who purchased it for £5.

587165: At the Lower Lydbrook river road junction, go for 1 mile towards Coleford, then turn towards Eastbach. After 400 yards, take the forest track on the right. The tree can be found 300 yards on the right.

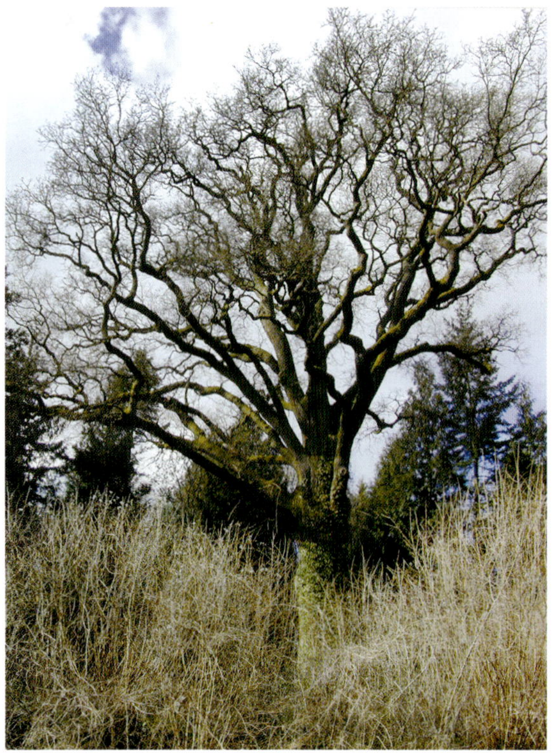

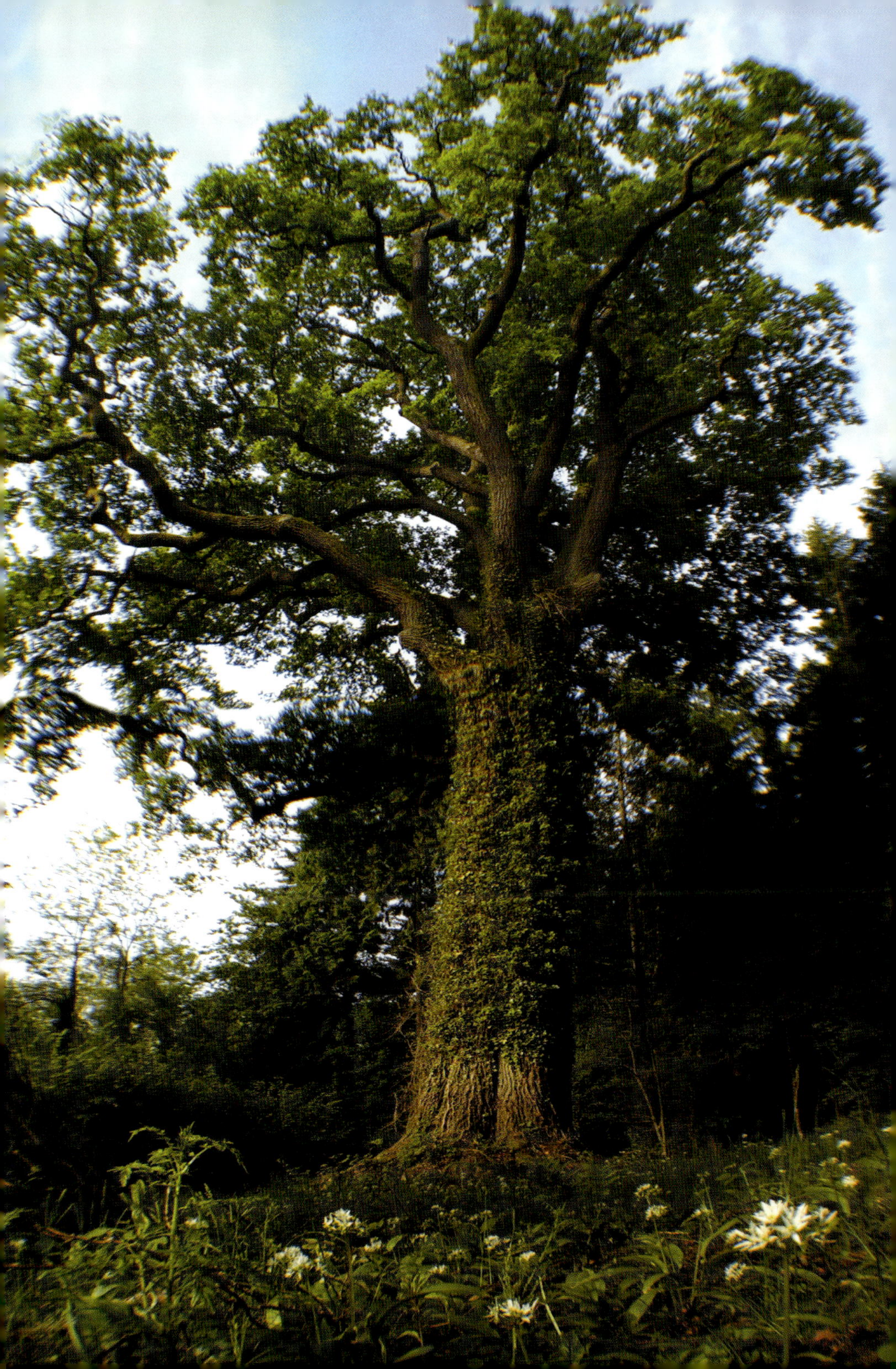

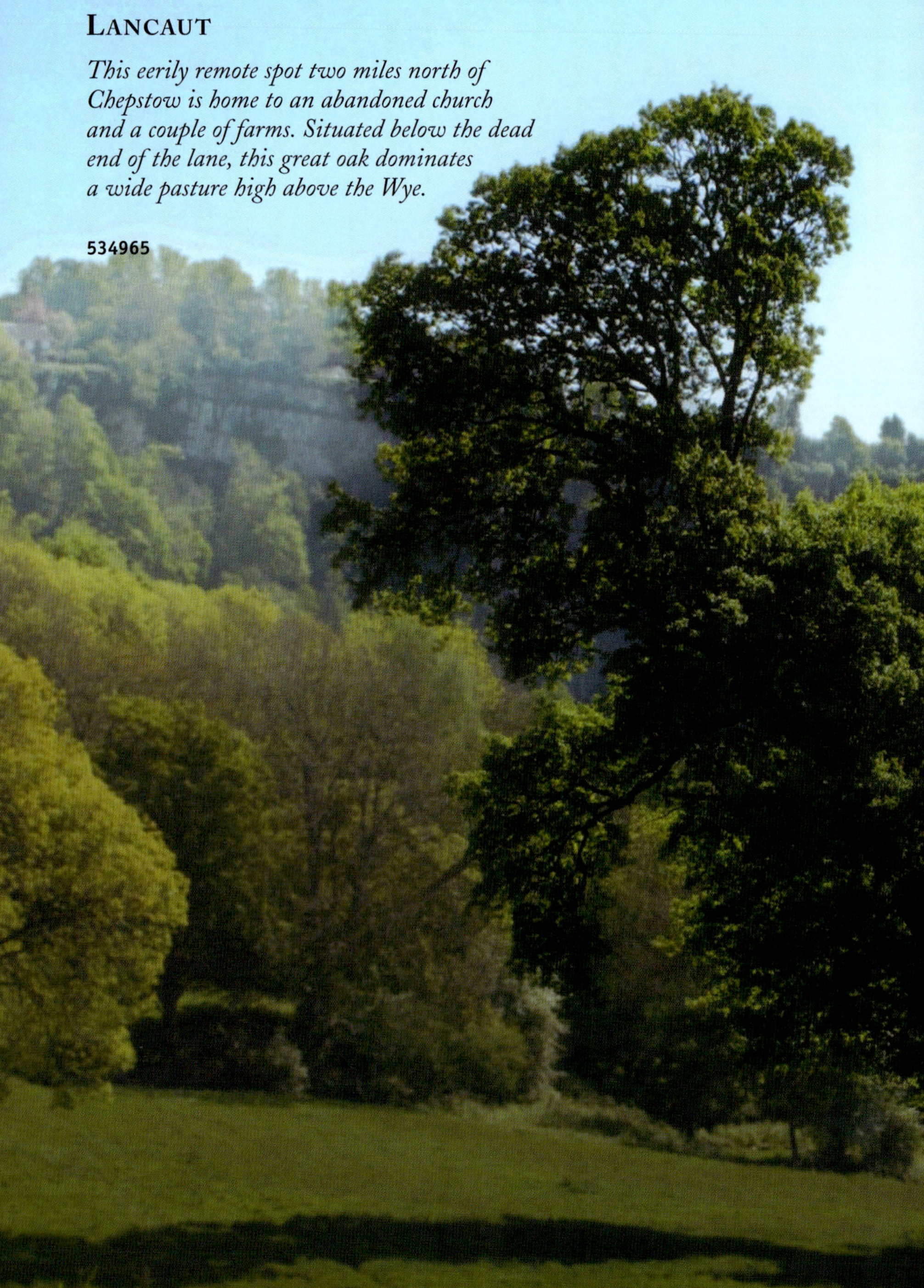

Lancaut

This eerily remote spot two miles north of
Chepstow is home to an abandoned church
and a couple of farms. Situated below the dead
end of the lane, this great oak dominates
a wide pasture high above the Wye.

534965

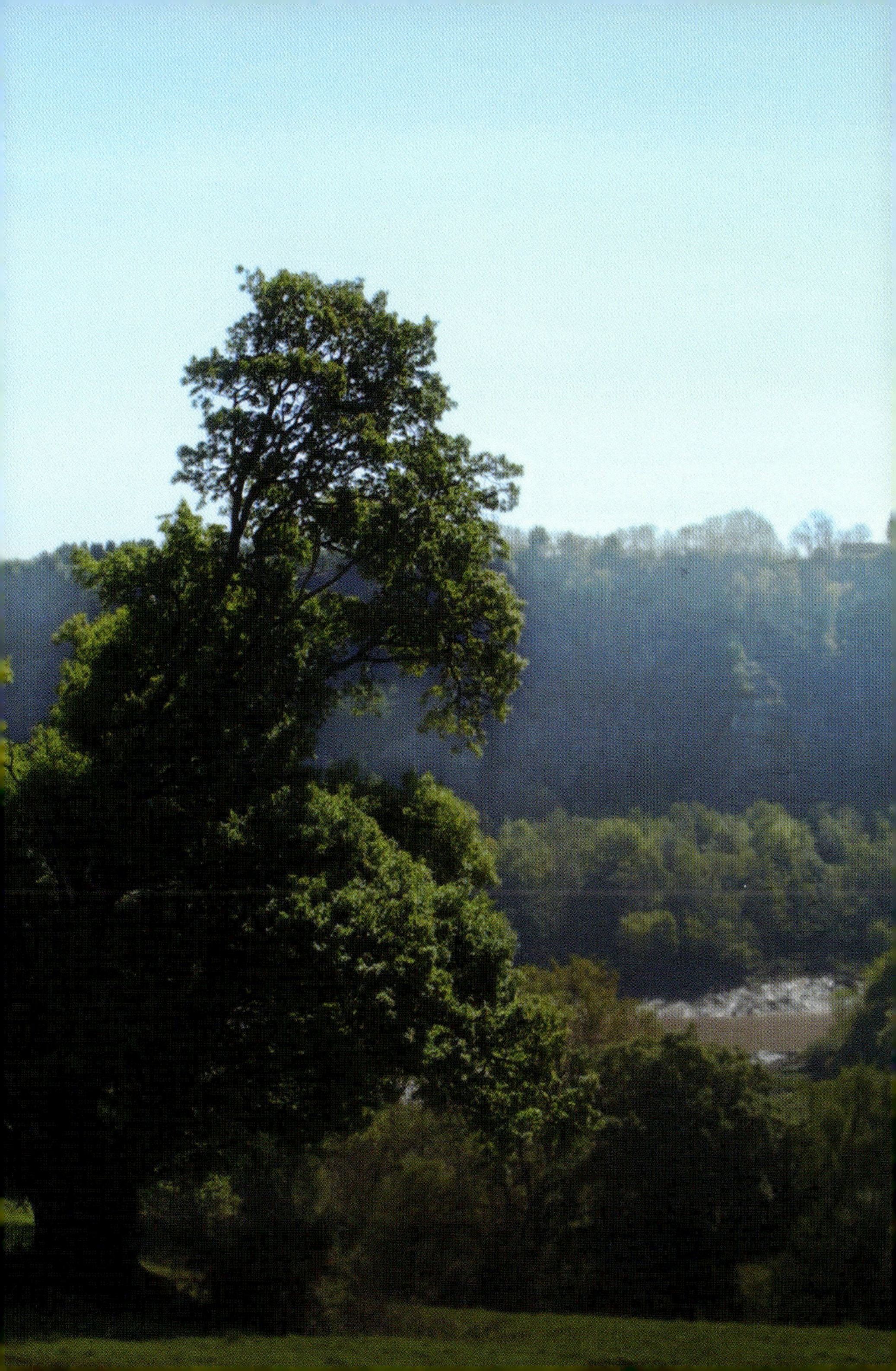

Machen oak

Edward Machen was Deputy Surveyor of Dean in the early nineteenth century and shouldered the responsibility for shipbuilding during the Napoleonic Wars and for the fleet's regeneration afterwards.

Machen lived at Eastbach Court and his oak stands nearby on the high ridge north-east of Edge End. Its split trunk suggests that it was once pollarded. It seems in good health despite the evidence of burning at the base of the trunk.

The Forestry Commission's ban on fires in the woods includes picnic and camp sites.

596136: From the Eastbach turning on the A4136, drive a quarter of a mile towards Coleford, then take the tarmac entry on the right. Immediately turn left, stop after 100 yards. Machen is just ahead.

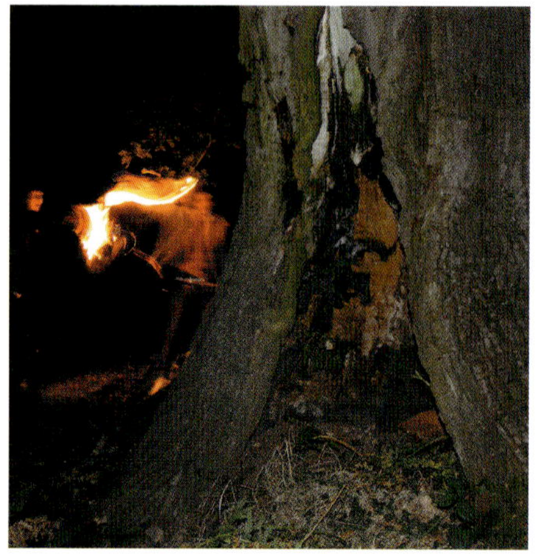

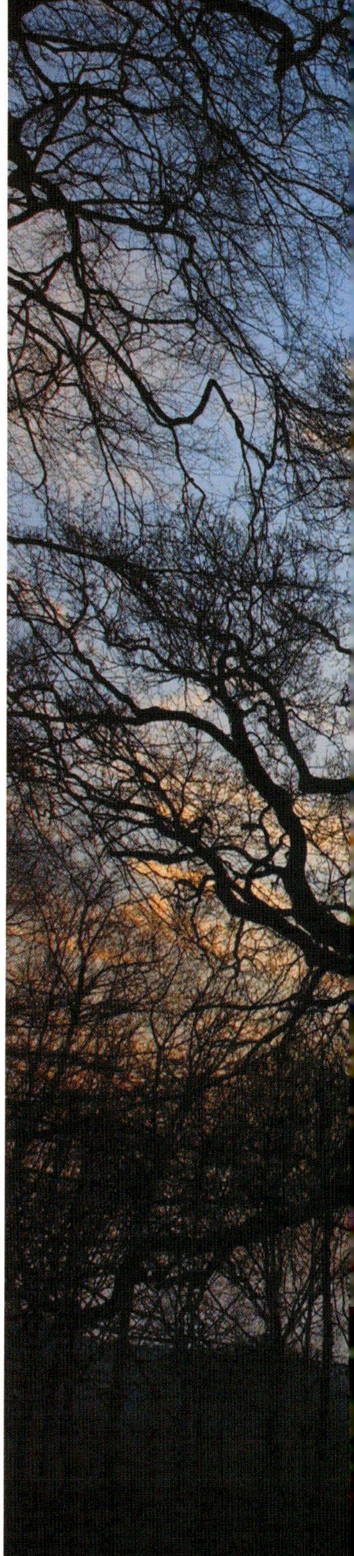

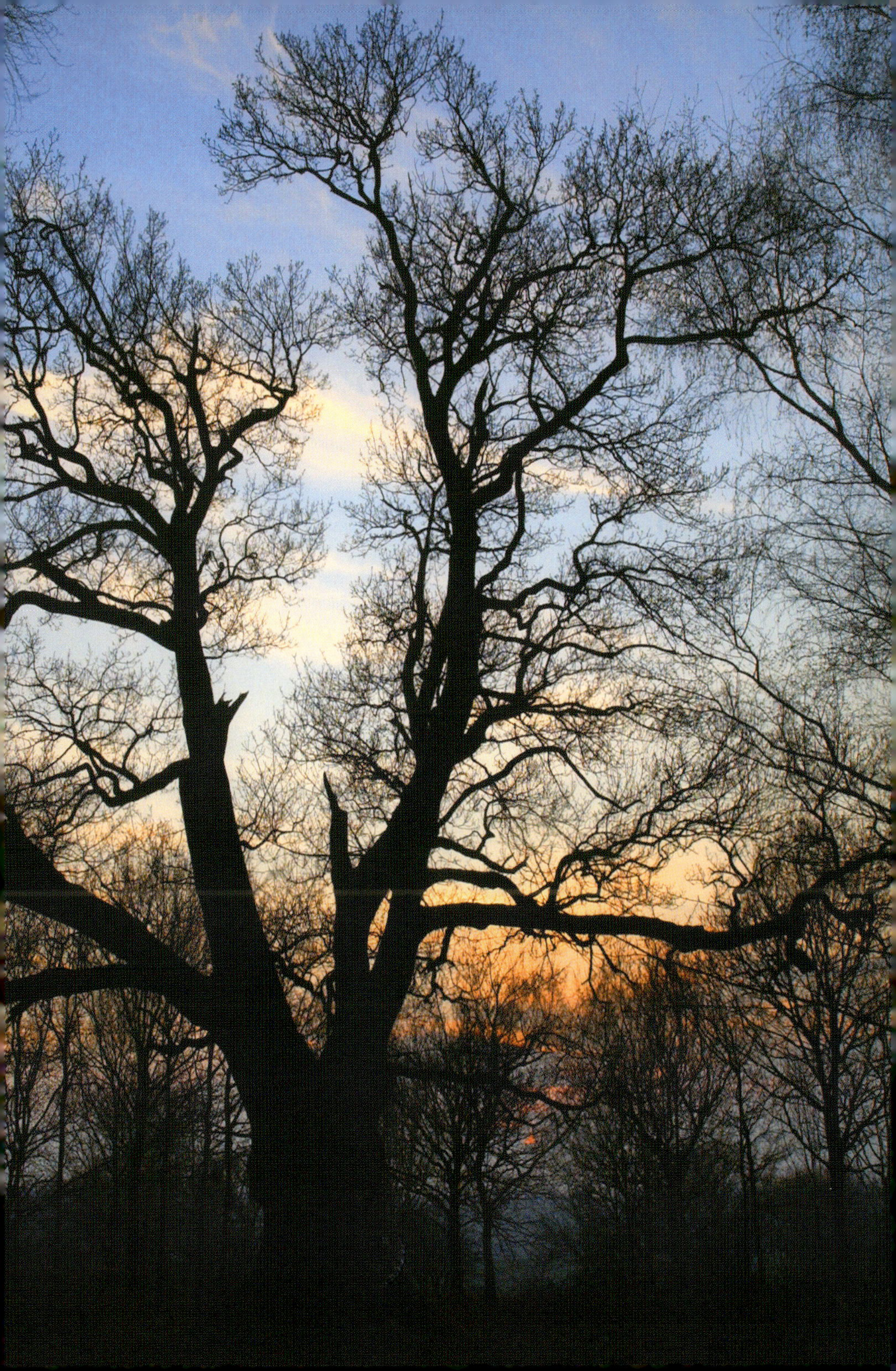

GOING, GONE

Forest records dated 1282 show Kaderickes oak marked on the spot of today's Crad oak (below). About 300 years old, it rears up defiantly from its clearing. Sadly it is now on its last legs, appearing to lean into the surrounding trees for support.

607139: From the Lydbrook/Lydney junction of the A4136, go uphill for 400 yards towards Monmouth, turn left into Forest Road. At the barrier, turn left and head downhill for 300 yards.

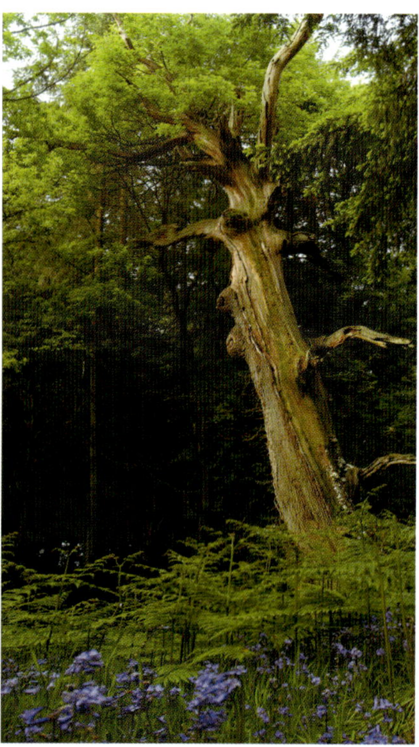

Since 1956, all that remains of Newland's great oak (opposite) is a huge stump in a field with a young tree, raised from a cutting, growing beside it. Pacing round the broken remains of the old tree suggests a circumference of 45–50 feet. The simple view of the old stump and the young oak sum up regeneration – a central theme for any forest and every forester.

552098: Take the lane to the north out of the village, park where a farm track leaves on the left. After a couple of hundred yards, the new young oak can be seen on the skyline of the meadow on the right.

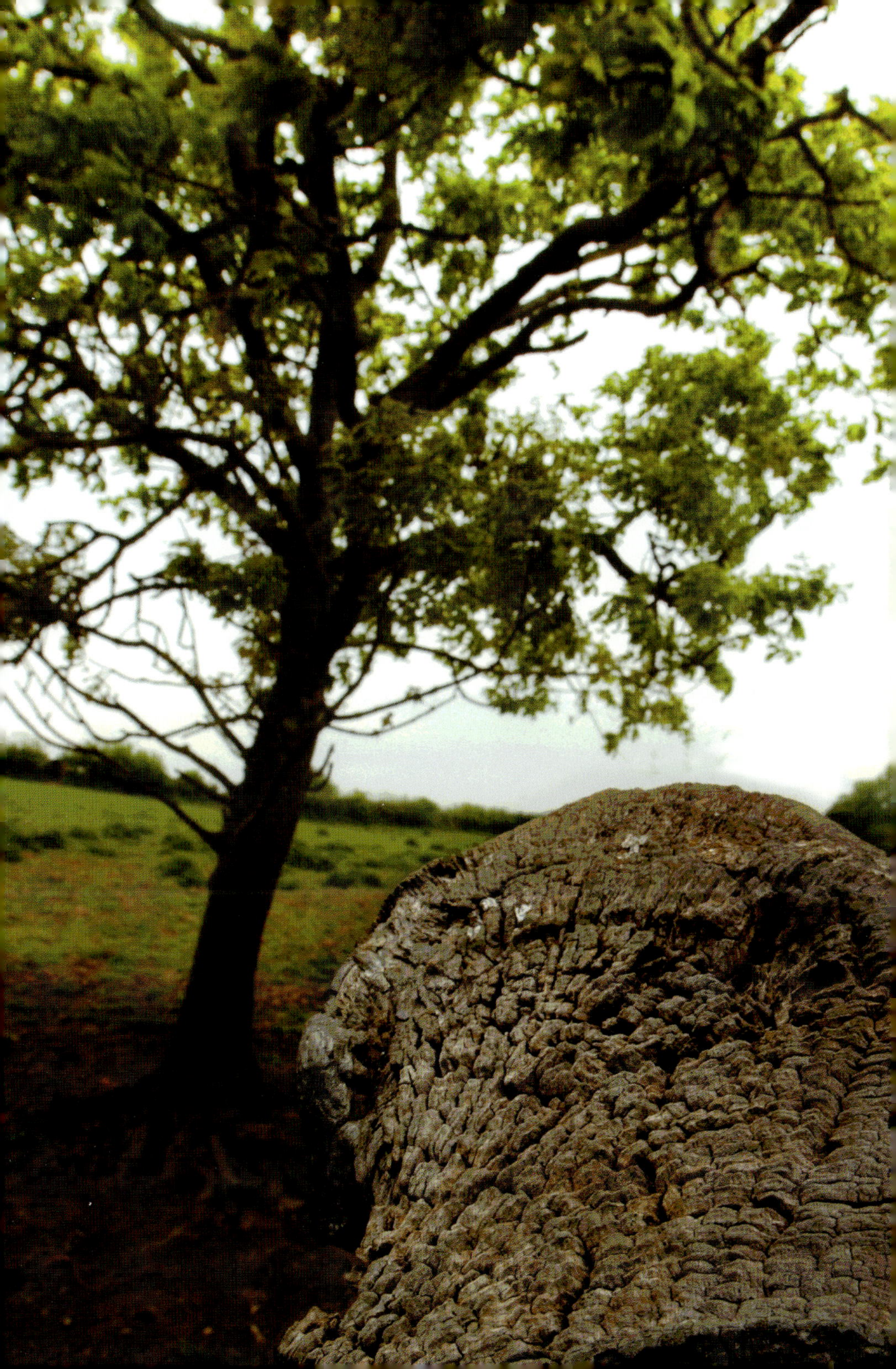

BLAISDON OAKS

Trees standing in fields are frequently the remains of ancient hedges. A swollen bole, or base of the trunk (below) suggests a tree that has been under stress. As a defence mechanism, growth is directed away from the high branches to conserve energy.

706175 (opposite); 715186 (below)

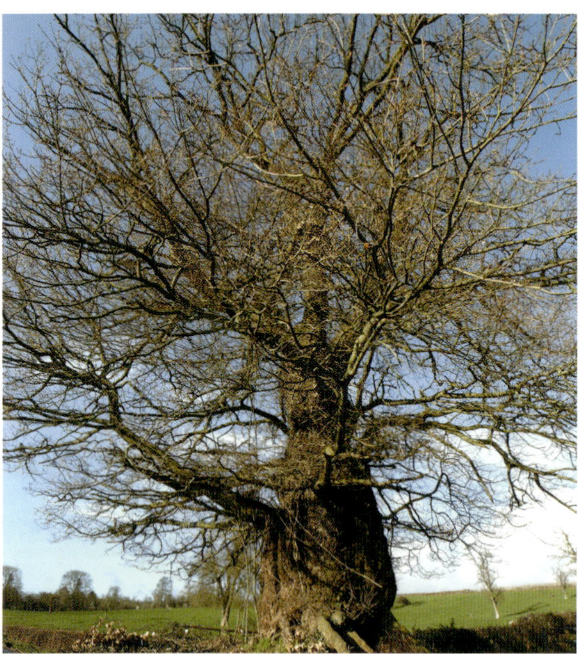

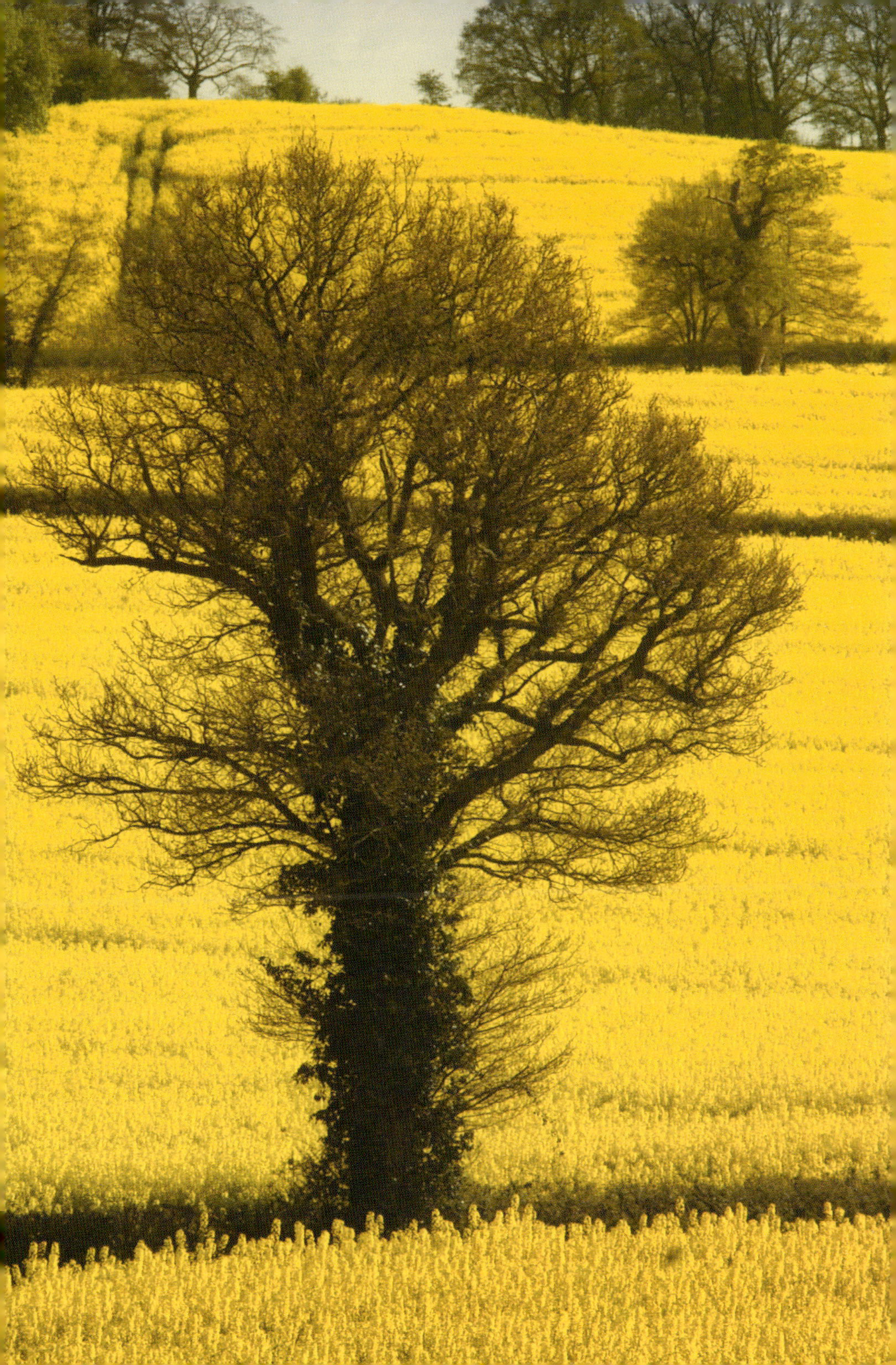

WOOLASTON OAKS

These two trees, one each side of the A48, both derive from hedgerows. They show different defences against stress: the tree in the sheep pasture (opposite) has directed its growth into a swollen bole (see page 26), while the other has allowed some of its high branches to die, putting its energy into lower growth – an effect known as 'stag-headed'.

Below right: A swelling known as a burr develops to help heal a wound, such as a torn-off branch, or to fight infection. The compex grained wood of a burr is valued by furniture makers.

593993 (opposite); 571975 (below)

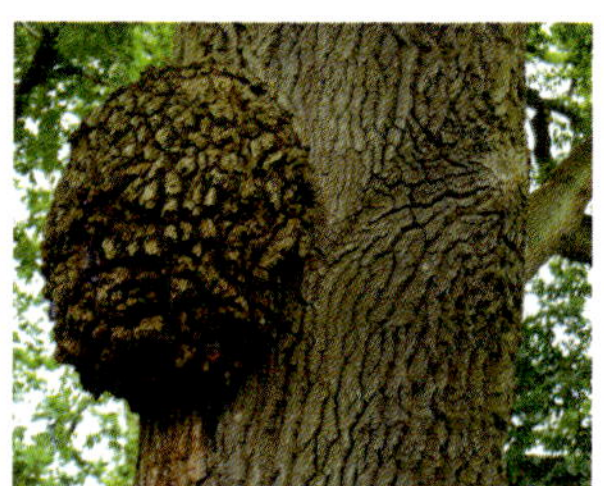

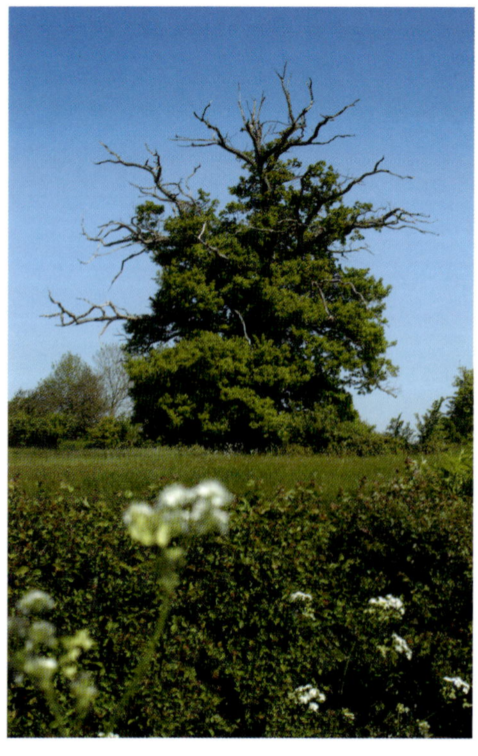

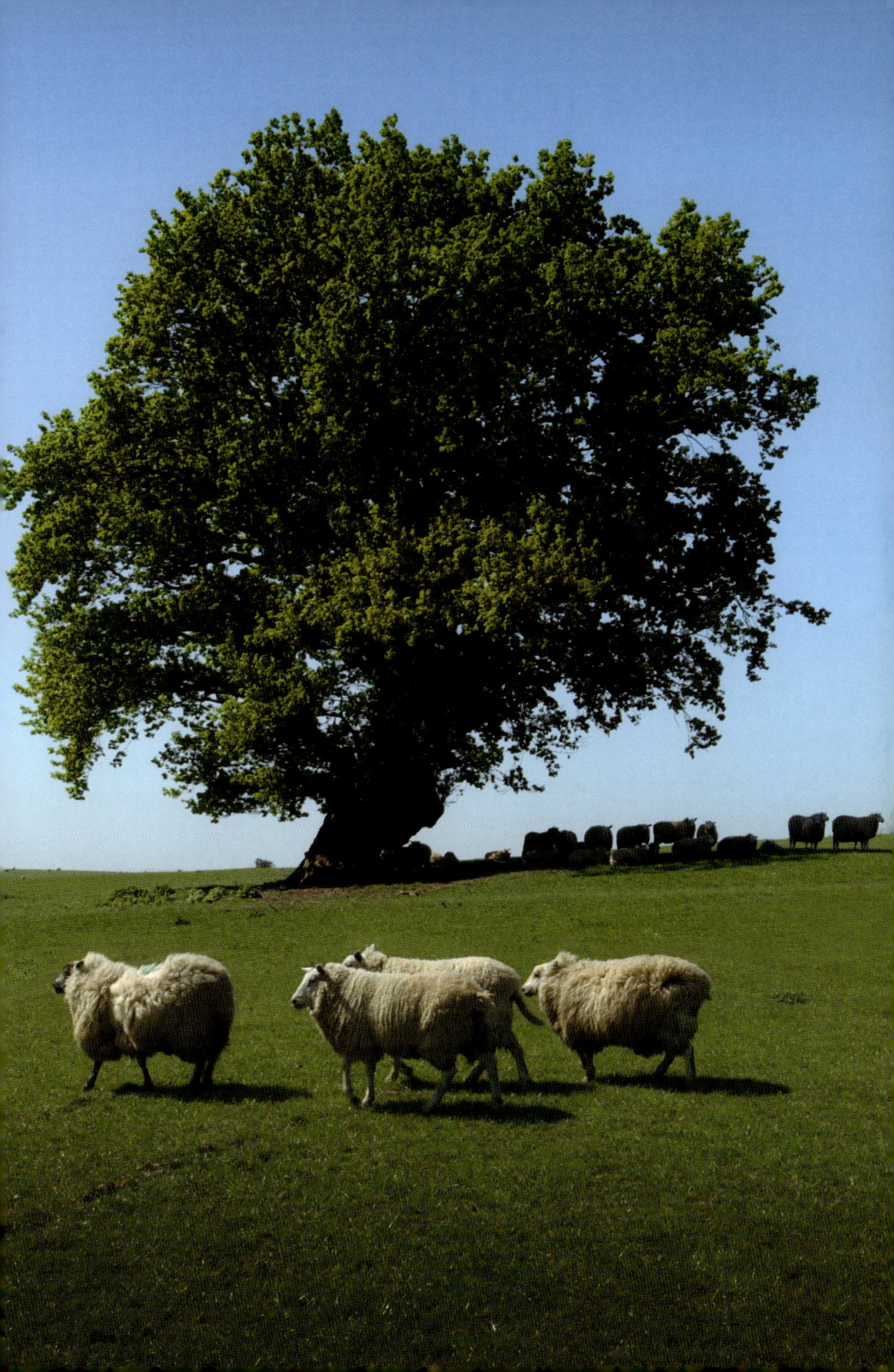

ROYAL OAKS

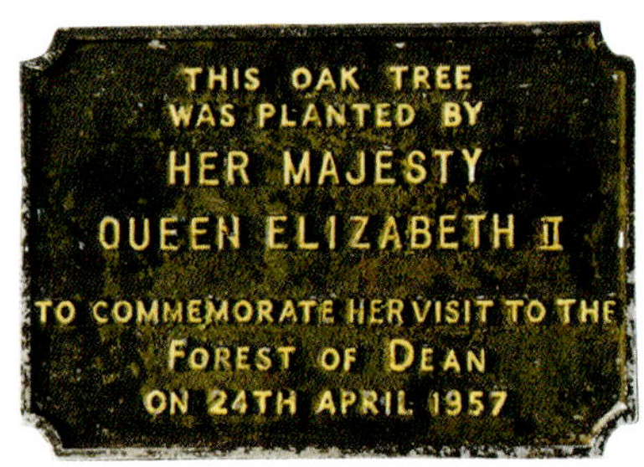

*Three commemorative trees
form a line across the road
towards New Fancy, opposite
Speech House. The one nearest
the main road is in memory of
Prince Albert and is dated
1861; the other two were
planted by Queen Elizabeth II
and Prince Philp in 1957.
Albert's tree was grown from an acorn of an oak
planted by Elizabeth I in Panshager Park,
Hertfordshire. Reputedly, the present Queen's tree
was raised from an acorn of Albert's, providing
four centuries of continuity between
the two monarchs.*

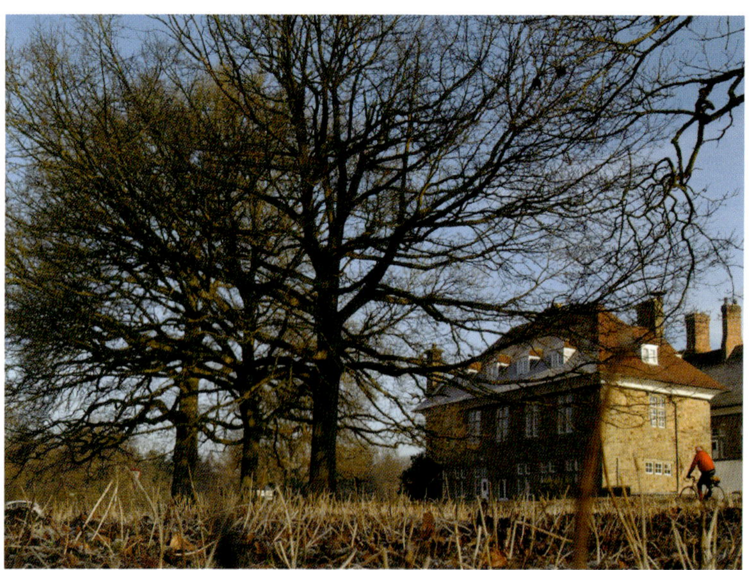

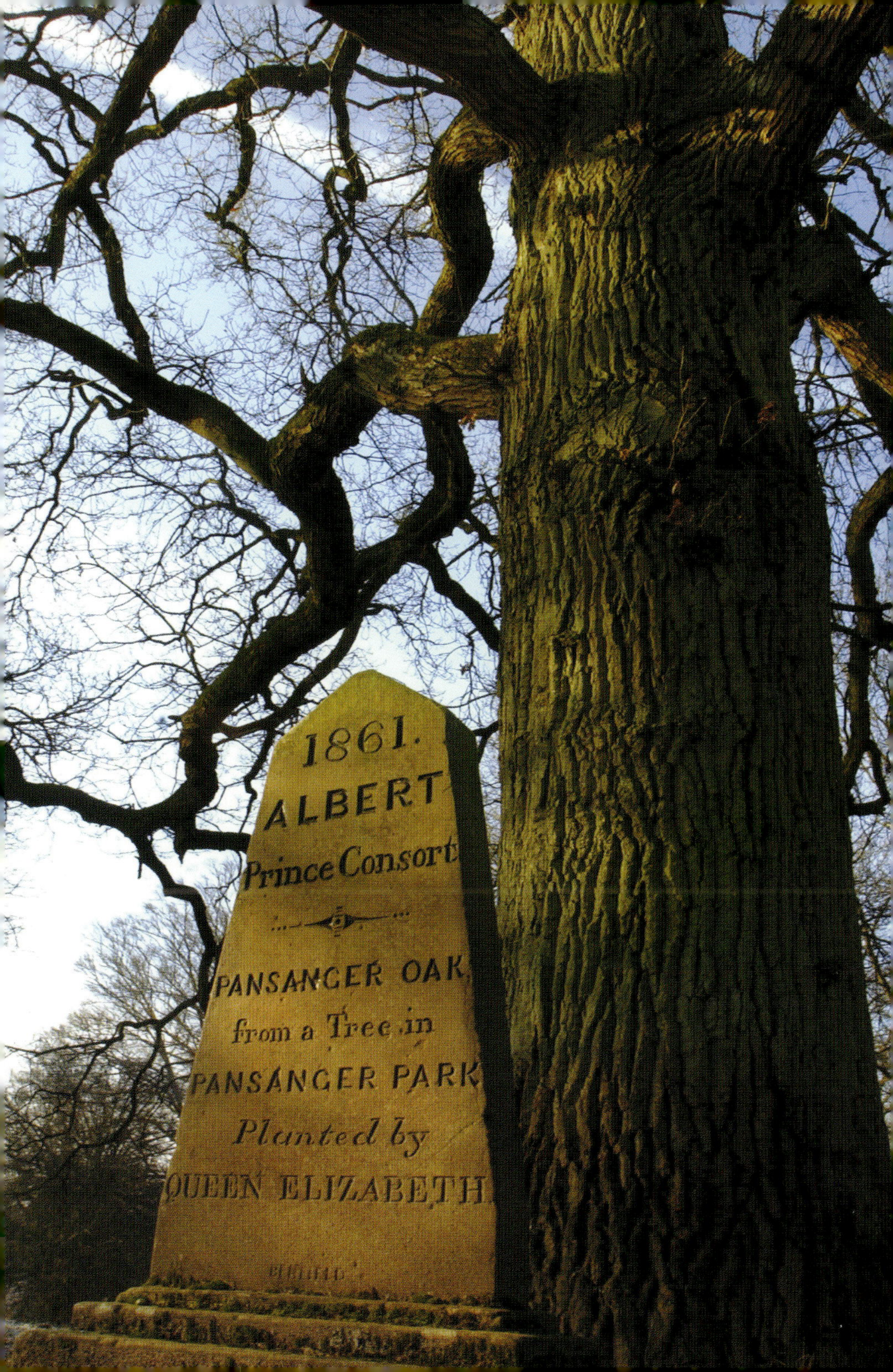

1861.
ALBERT
Prince Consort
PANSANGER OAK,
from a Tree in
PANSANGER PARK
Planted by
QUEEN ELIZABETH

OAKS IN THE SNOW

A fine row of oaks lines the road between Cinderford Bridge and Dilke Hospital, the sculptural quality of their bare limbs emphasised by the snow. Another dramatic specimen (below) stands by the A4136, just below Plump Hill summit towards Nailbridge.

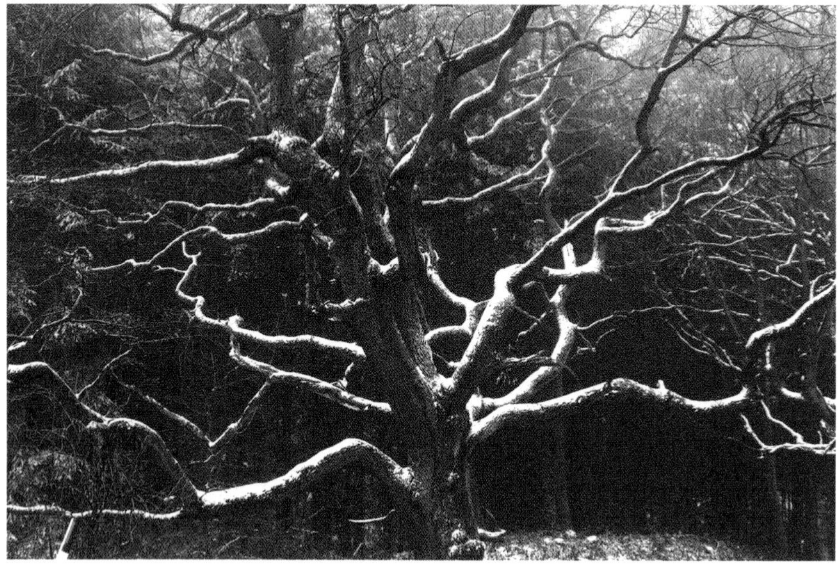

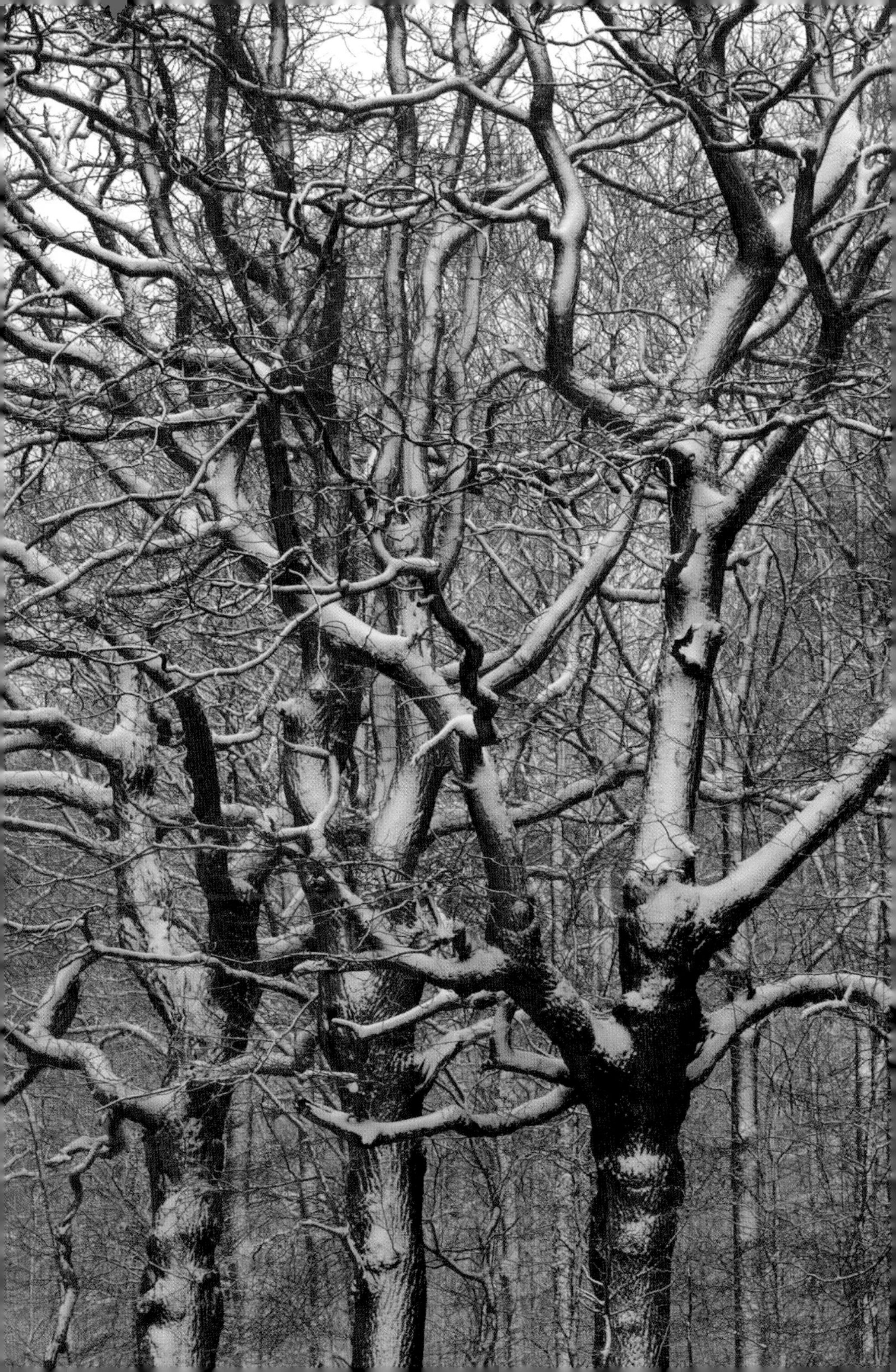

OAKLANDS

The mansion at Oaklands Park was built for ironmaster Richard Crawshay in the early nineteenth century. The name predated the house and referred to woods on the estate where oaks were grown as a crop for use in shipbuilding and construction. Forester Nick Assirati, who manages the estate for the Steiner Community, shows a typical example of a woodland oak with a straight trunk and curving upper branches.

In contrast is a parkland tree (below) whose branches, with no constriction from competing trees, can spread freely from the start. (See also pages 58 and 74.)

Oaklands Park is private, but some sections are visible from public paths.

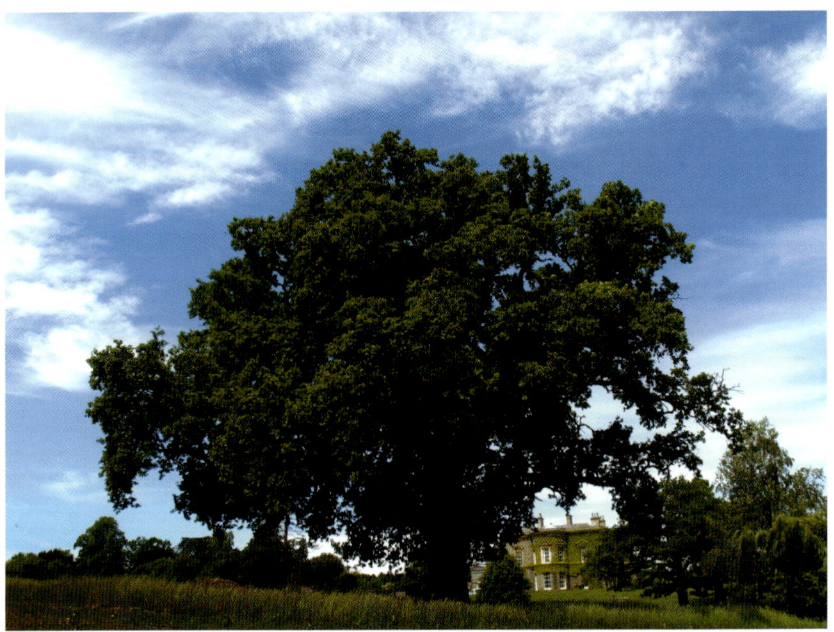

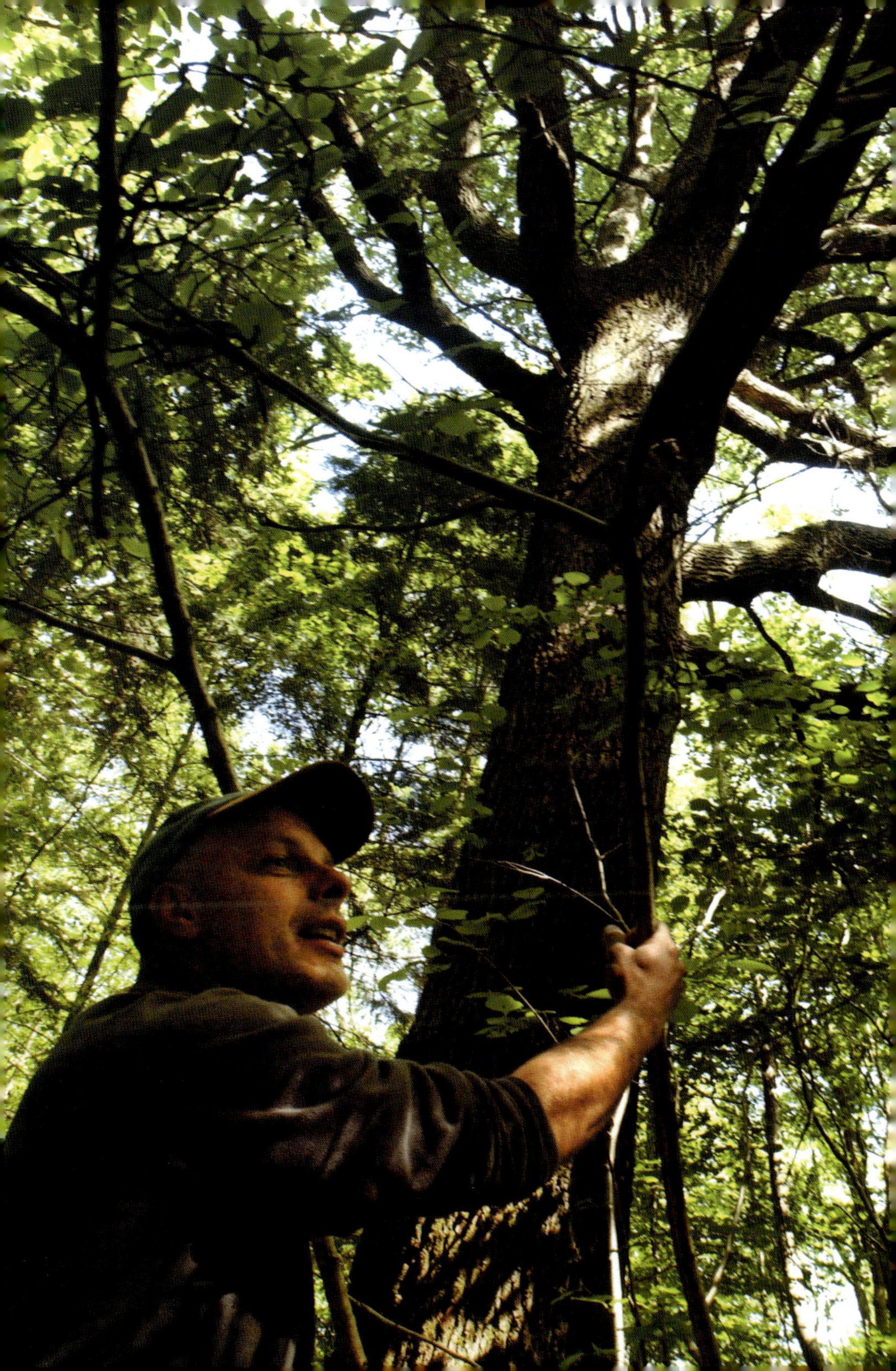

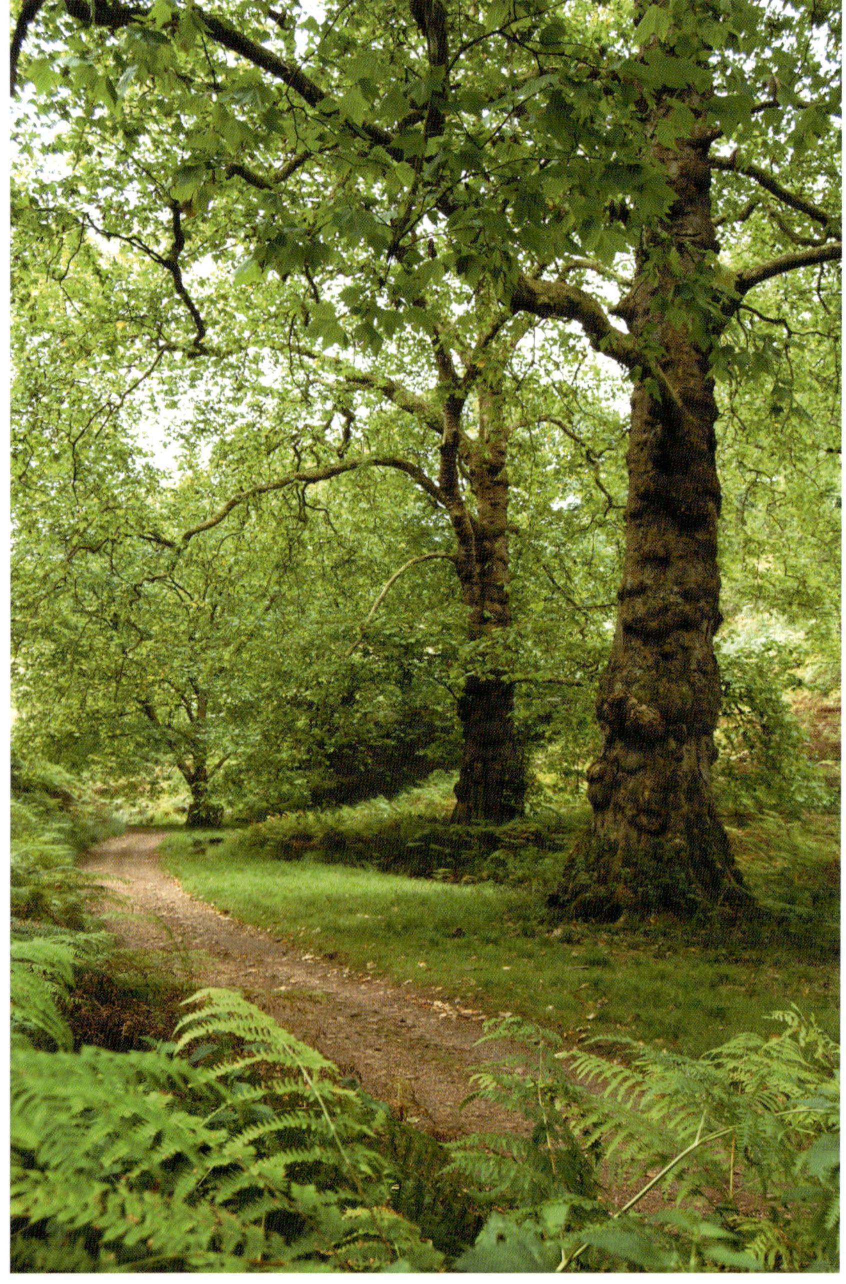

2

CHAMPIONS

(AND CONTENDERS)

Many trees in the Forest are celebrated as the oldest, biggest or tallest in Dean, or even in the whole country. In the forestry business they are known as 'champions'. The other trees in this chapter are worthy contenders, even if only for our interest.

The Forest of Dean is renowned for its ancient role of providing oak trees for industry. By the end of the nineteenth century the situation became reversed as industry, particularly coal mining, practically overtook the Forest. Visitors looking at the beautiful woodland scenery today find it hard to believe that Dean was a landscape of pithead rigs and smoking chimneys.

Oaks may be the flag we would fly for Dean, as the title of this book suggests, but many other species also claim our interest. The Forestry Commission has to make a profit, and over the decades this has meant planting fast-growing conifers for rapid harvests. These have always been disguised with broad-leaved fringes to the edges of woods along the roads, and increasingly these non-conifers are valued for their own sake, as part of a policy to move the Forest towards a more natural landscape. Within the Forestry plantations are beech and oak woods, and on newly felled sections there are frequently single trees left standing – yews, larch, chestnut or any other tree of particular interest. In the centre of the Forest an arboretum contains an even more exotic mix of species.

The Forest's private estates, perhaps less subject to commercial pressures, also have a treasure trove of old and celebrated trees. Oaklands has an area dedicated to the maintenance and renewal of ancient oaks, which were grown as an industrial crop. This wood merges with planting originating from the nineteenth century, and a wide range of species are combined with the native beech and oak. Lydney Park (opposite), home to Lord Bledisloe, has a considerable acreage split between commercial forest, parkland, and woodland gardens.

FOREST FIRS

Most of the forest consists of planted conifers. The overview below is taken from Staple Edge. Outstanding examples that go beyond the easy perception of quick crop trees, are the four Weymouth pine in Sallowvallets – the oldest conifers in Dean, with the tallest over 130 feet high – and a grove of Douglas firs near Soudley, some over 145 feet.

605127 (Weymouth pines): From the entrance to the Cannop cycle centre, bear right, leaving the depot to your left. Ignore a track to the left and then one to the right; after a further 100 yards, turn left from the track following a stream valley. The pines are across a further track.

657108 (Douglas firs): Take the Littledean road from Soudley for 400 yards. At the track crossing, turn left and immediately left again for about 100 yards.

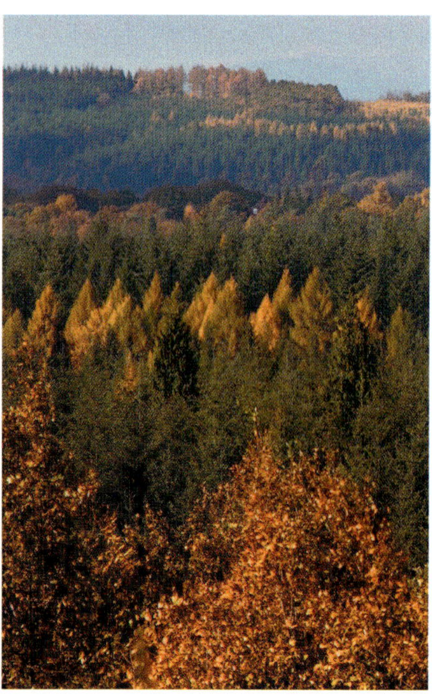

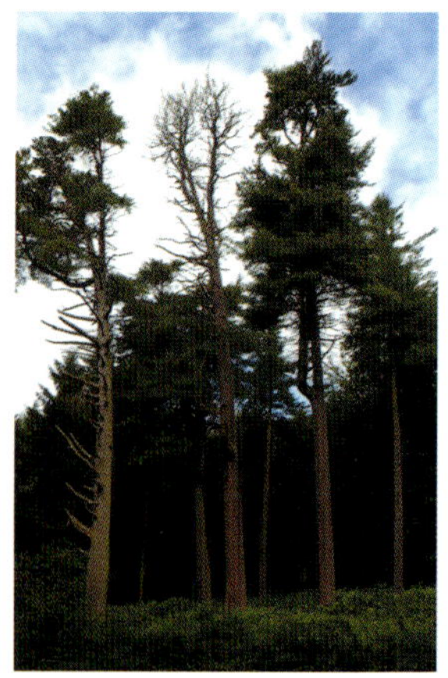

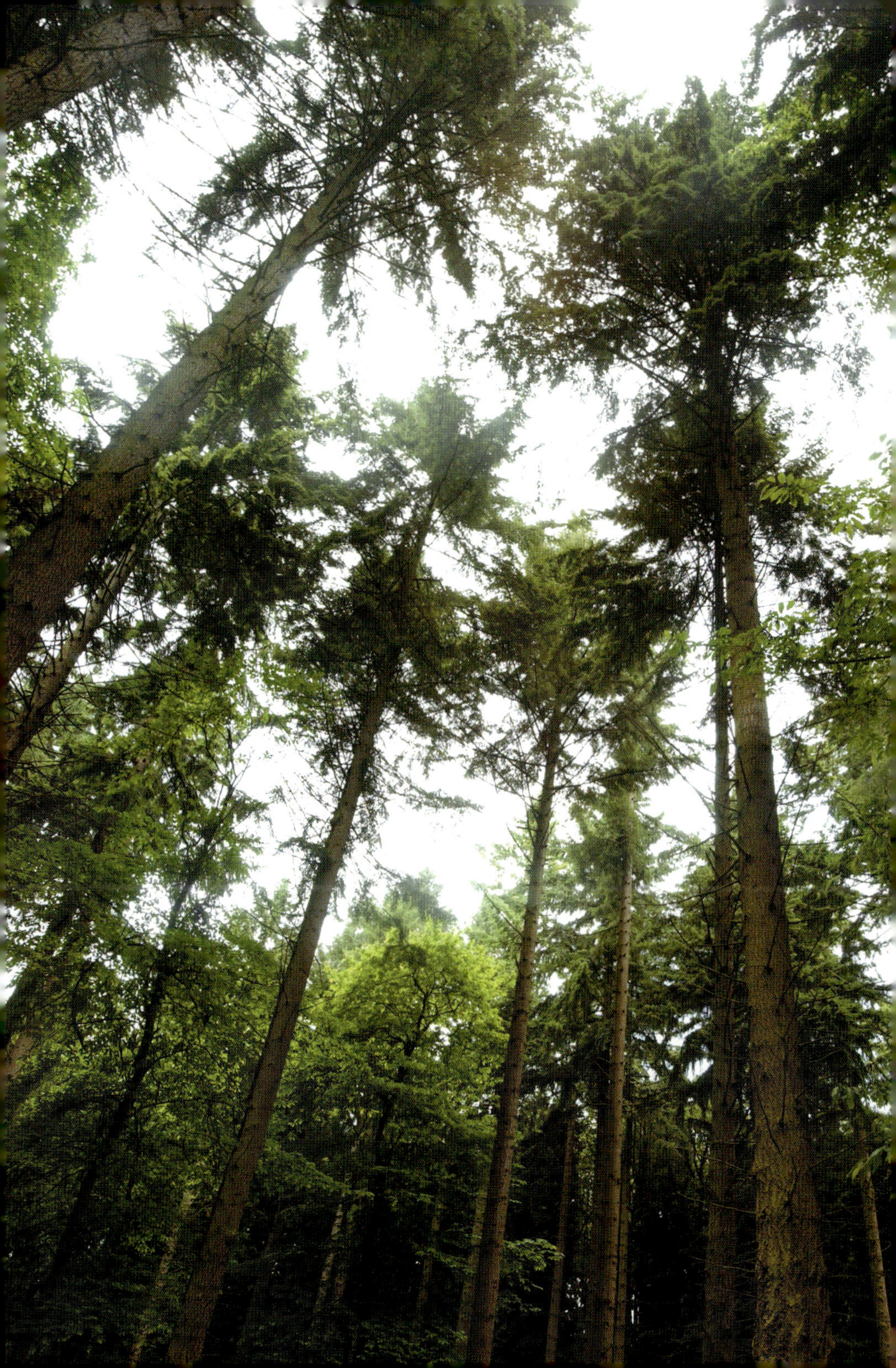

Bracelands Larch

At 16 tons, this tree is the largest conifer (by volume) in the Forest. The frosted saplings below are also larch, as is the mature plantation at Lydney Park.

**556132 (Bracelands): Follow the track past the campsite.
625085 (Saplings): Just south of King Charles II oak.
See also map on page 72.**

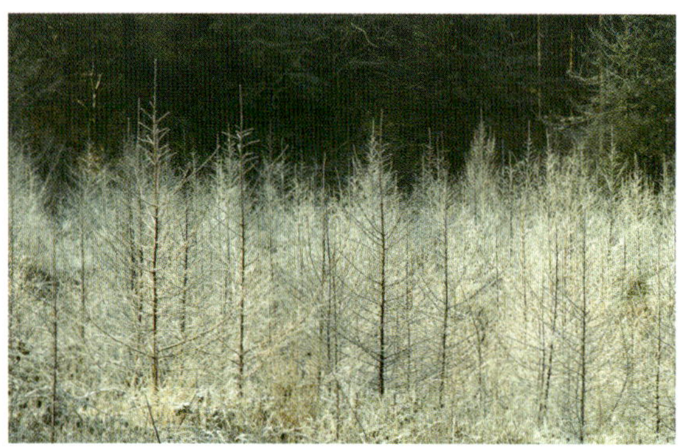

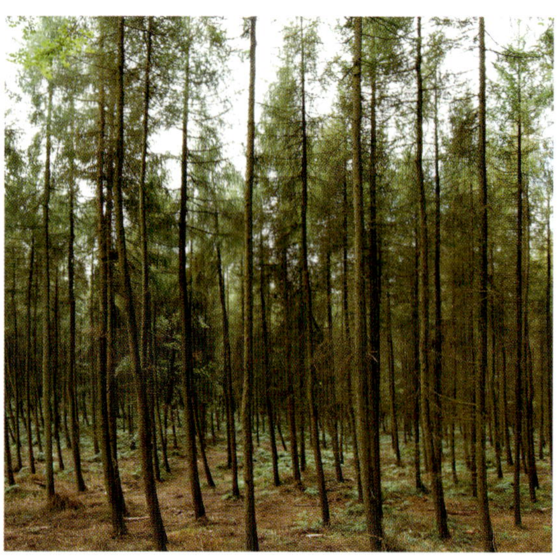

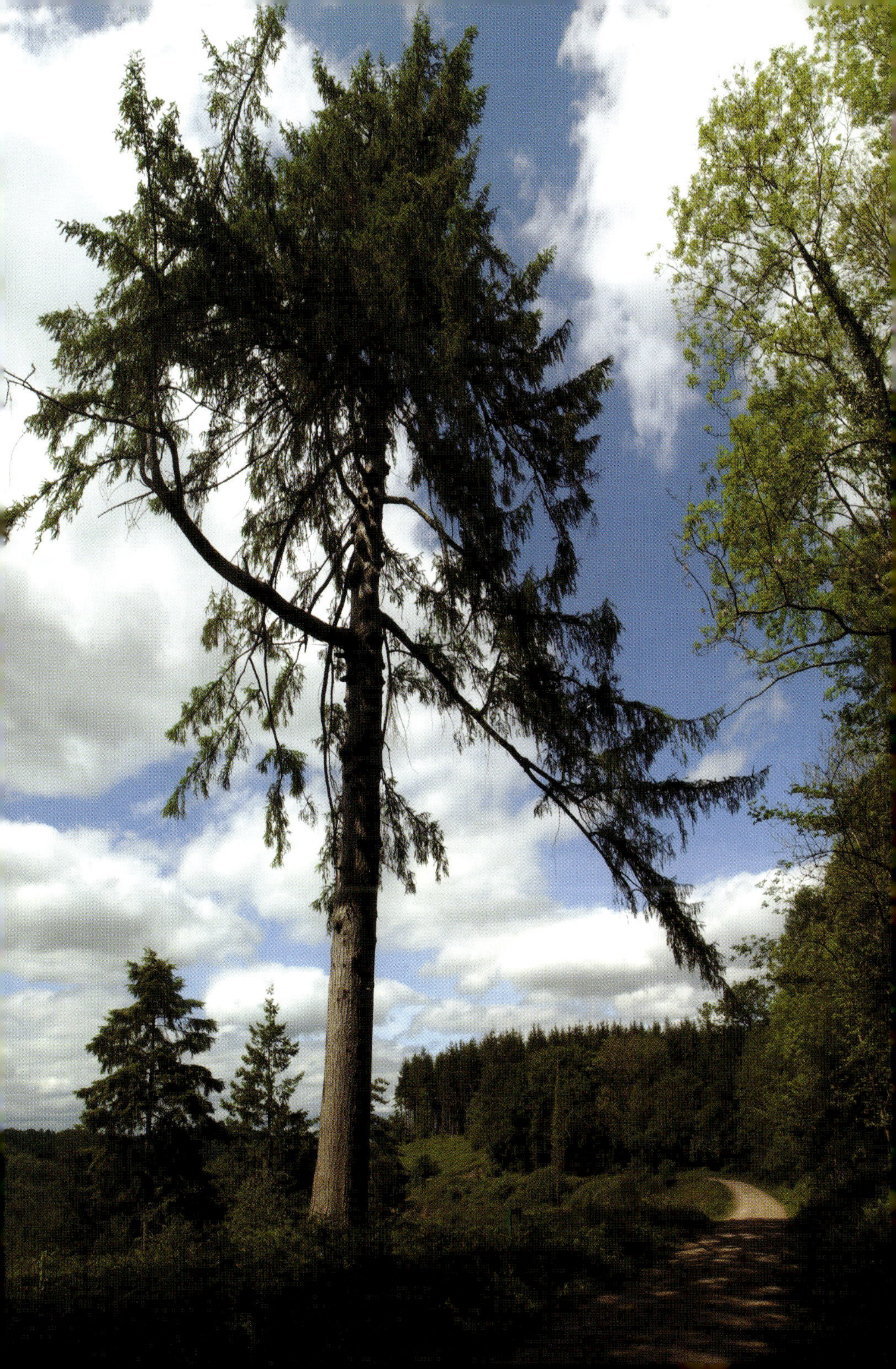

KING YEW

*This ancient tree is thought to be nearly 500 years
old. Its girth of 22 feet makes it the stoutest conifer
in Dean.*

**565002: Head south from Hewelsfied on the B4228.
At GR559002 (about a mile), take the forest track on the
left for 300 yards, bear left, then right, and after 25 yards
turn right to follow small path for about 150 yards.**

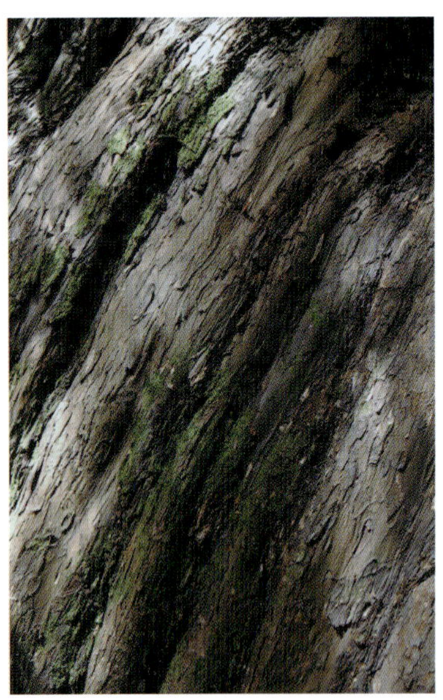

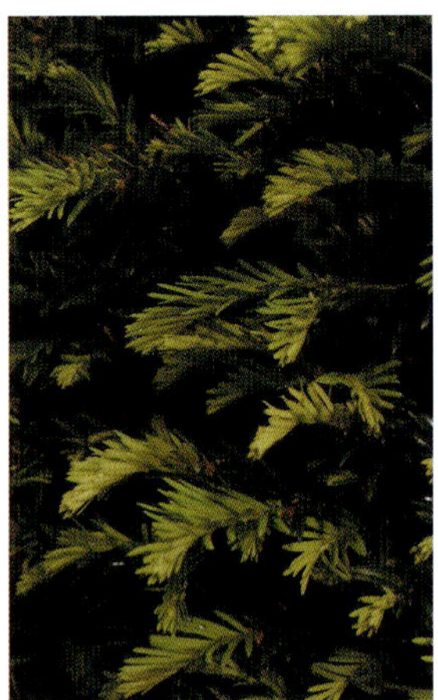

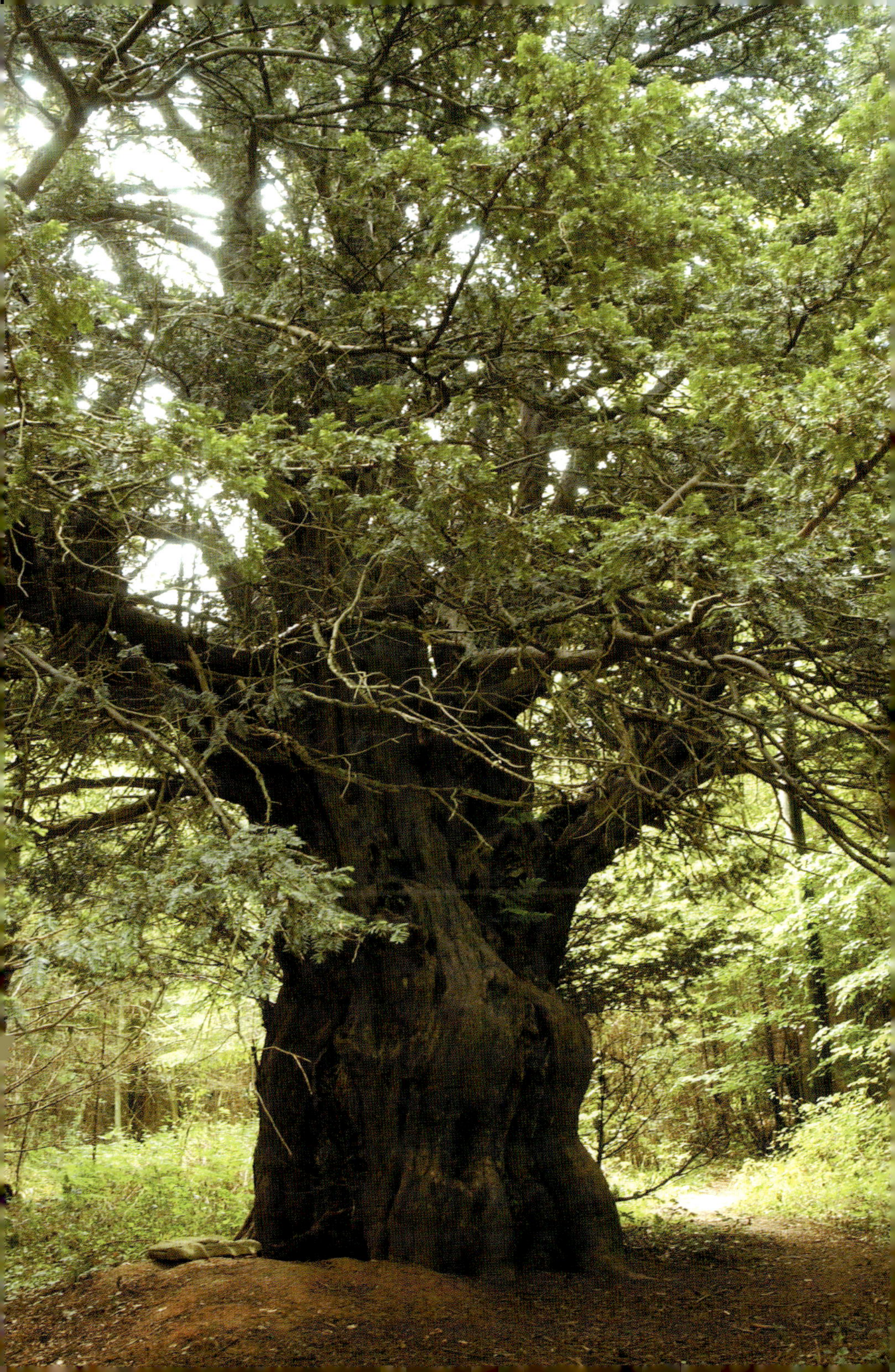

CHURCHYARD YEWS

Yews at Hewelsfield (below) and Woolaston (opposite) are possibly 800 years old, the most ancient trees in Dean. There is also an ancient yew at Awre.

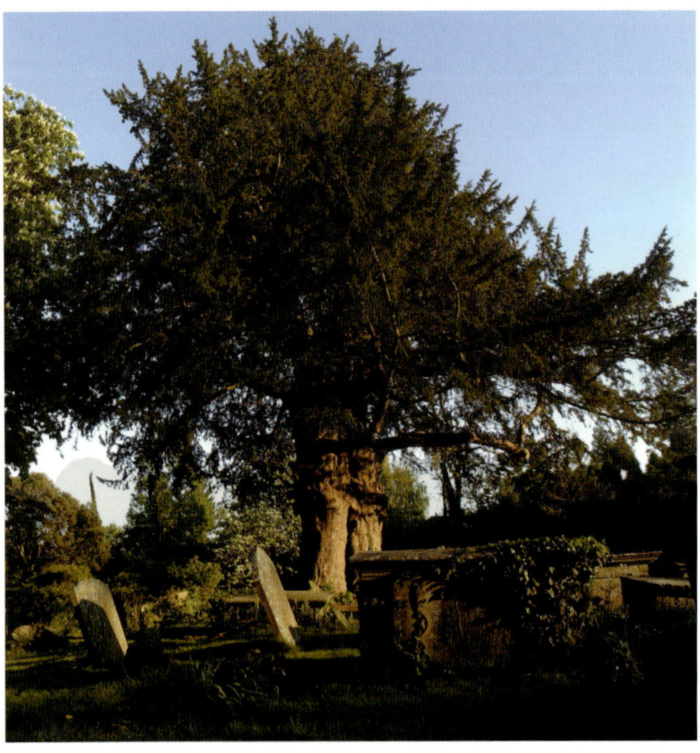

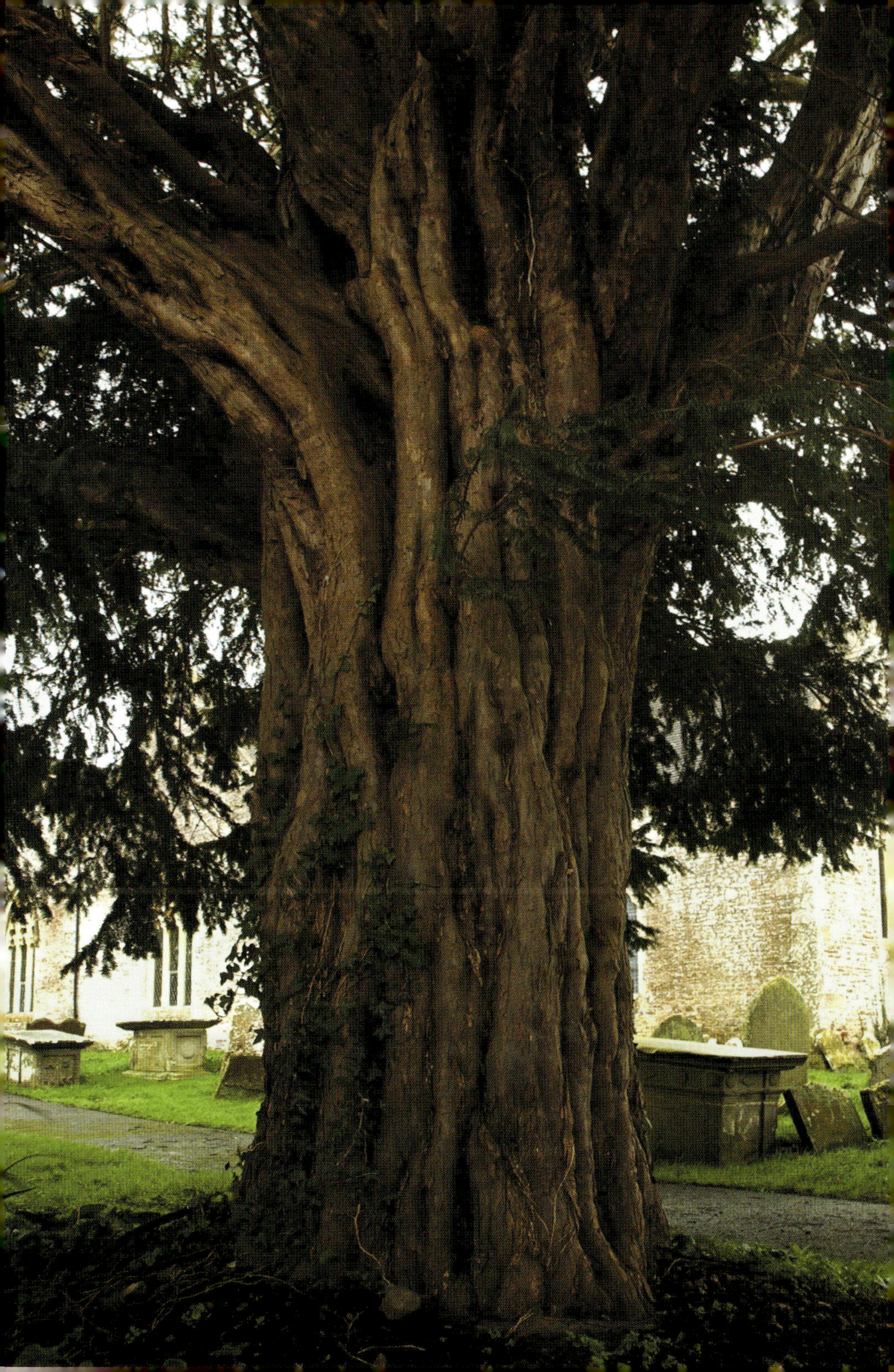

EDWARD VII YEWS

This commemorative set of yew trees stands directly opposite the front of Speech House.

Below: Snow on the branches makes following the path up from the Cannop Valley a tricky business for the author.

619120

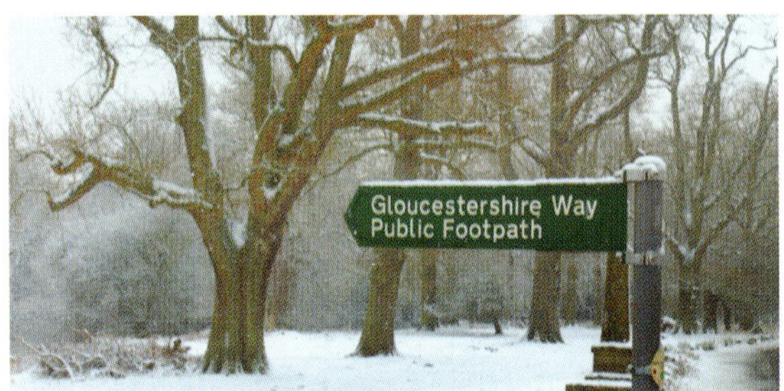

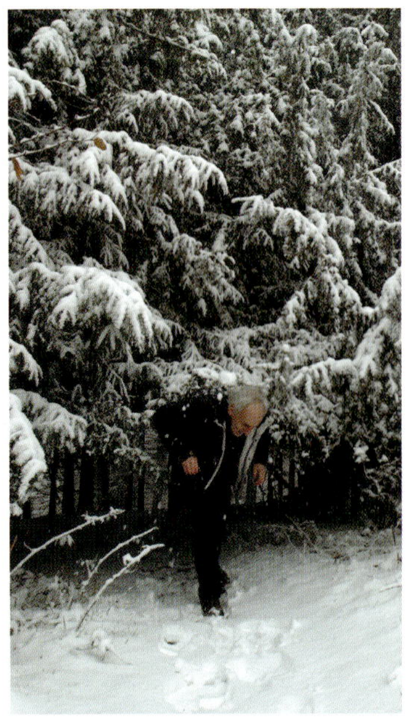

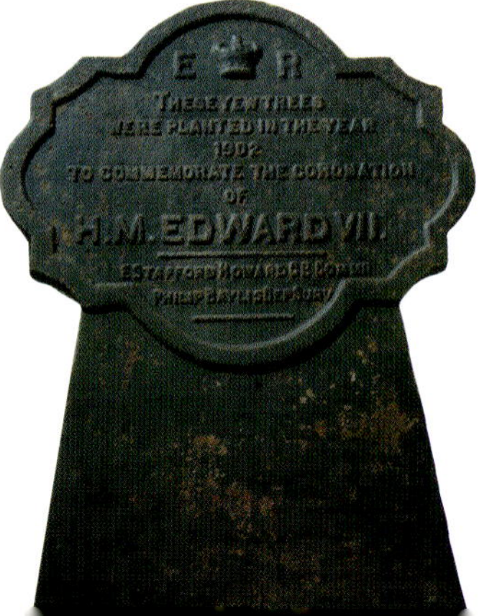

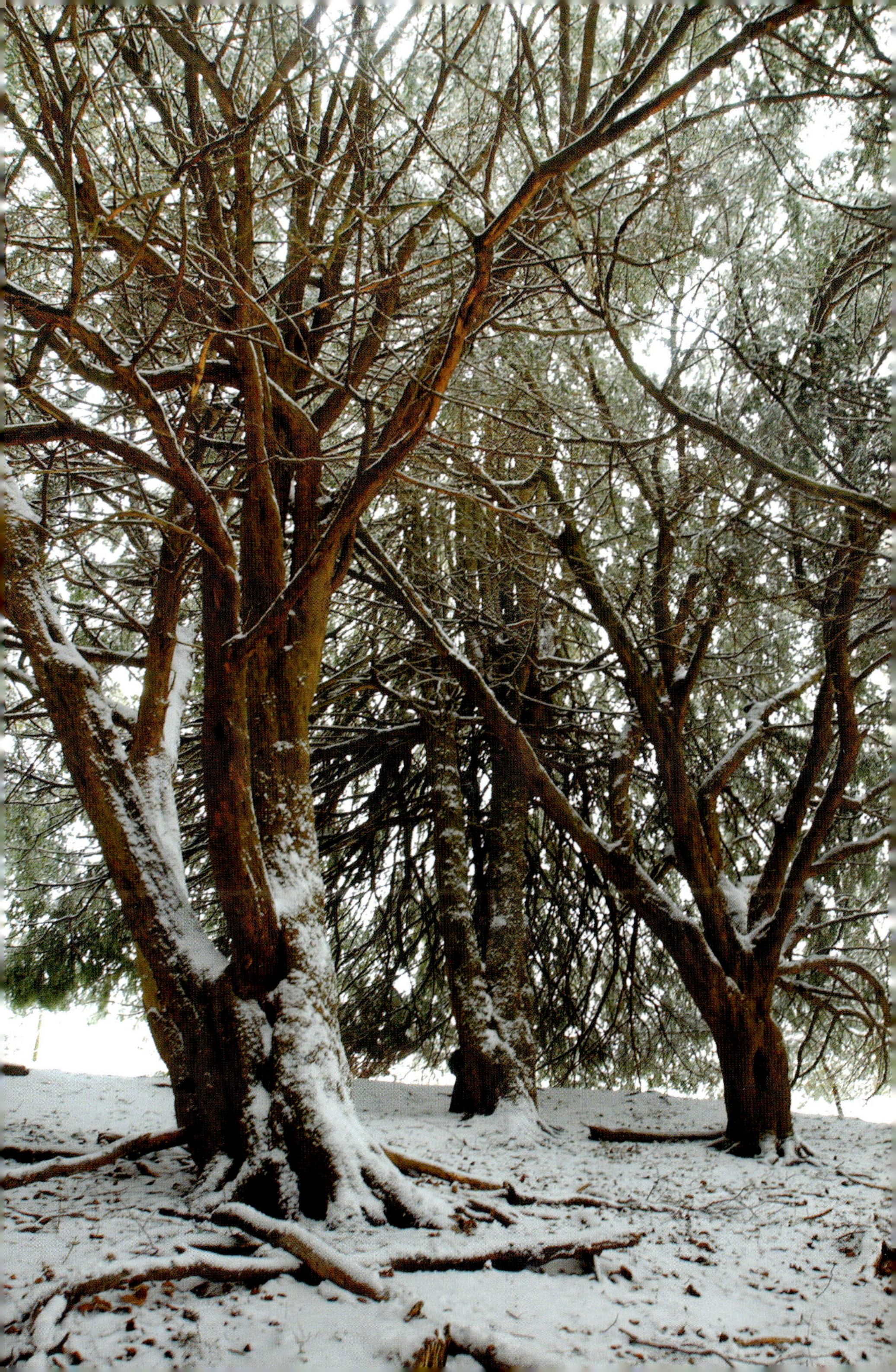

CYRIL HART ARBORETUM

This collection of rare and exotic species situated close to Speech House is named after Cyril Hart, whose research into Forest history and commitment to arboriculture did much to stimulate interest in Dean.

The contrasting conifers shown here are a Sequoia (opposite) and (below) a champion Cilician fir.

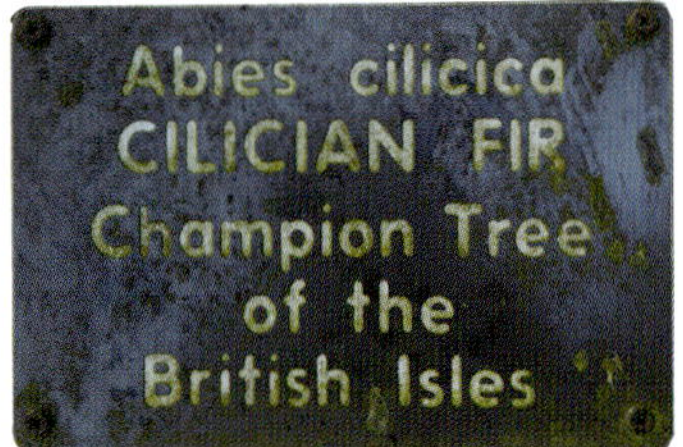

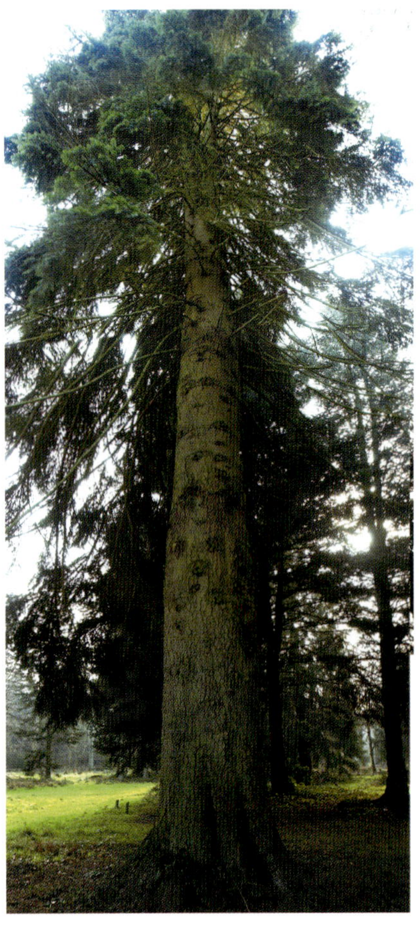

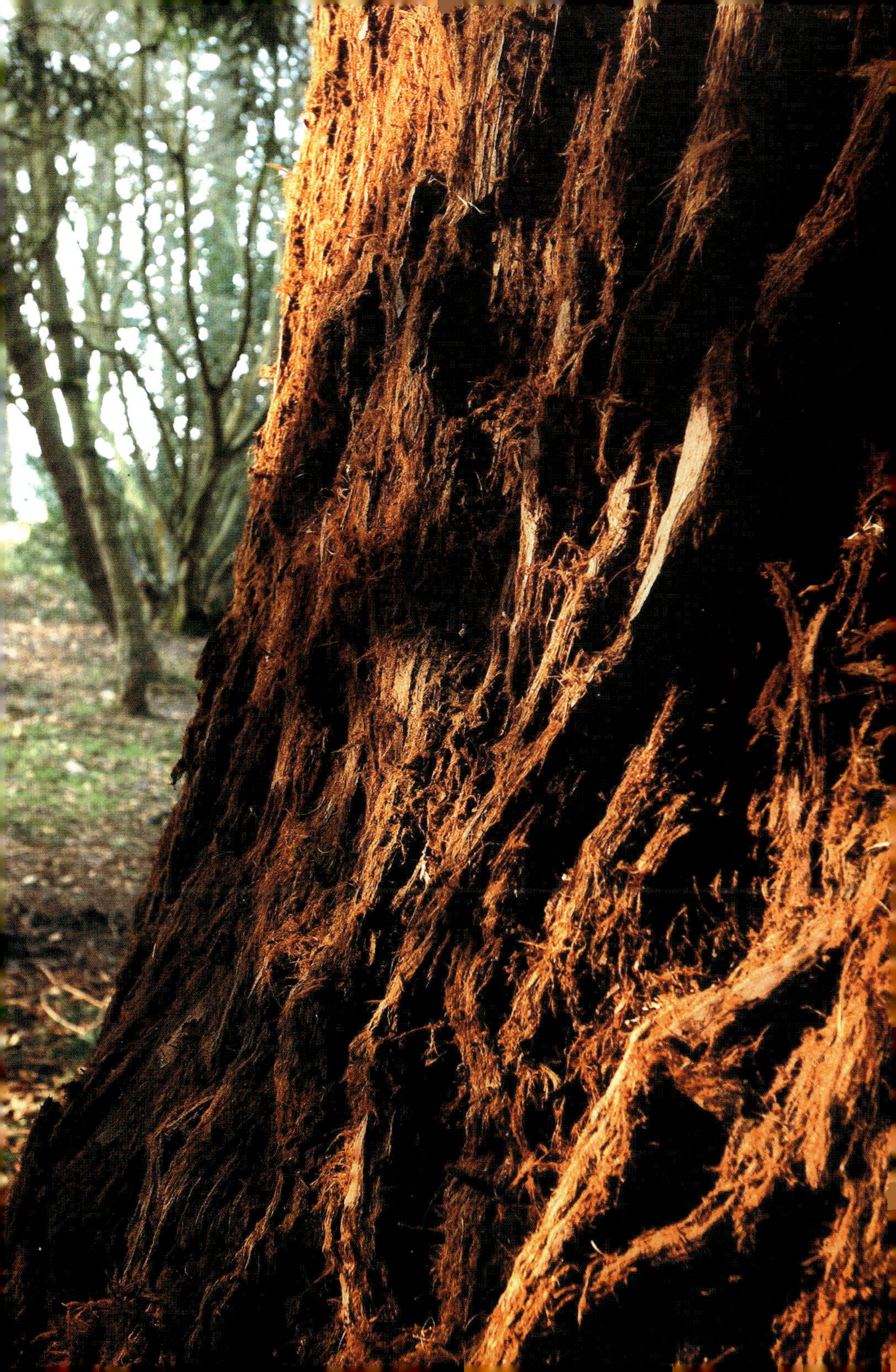

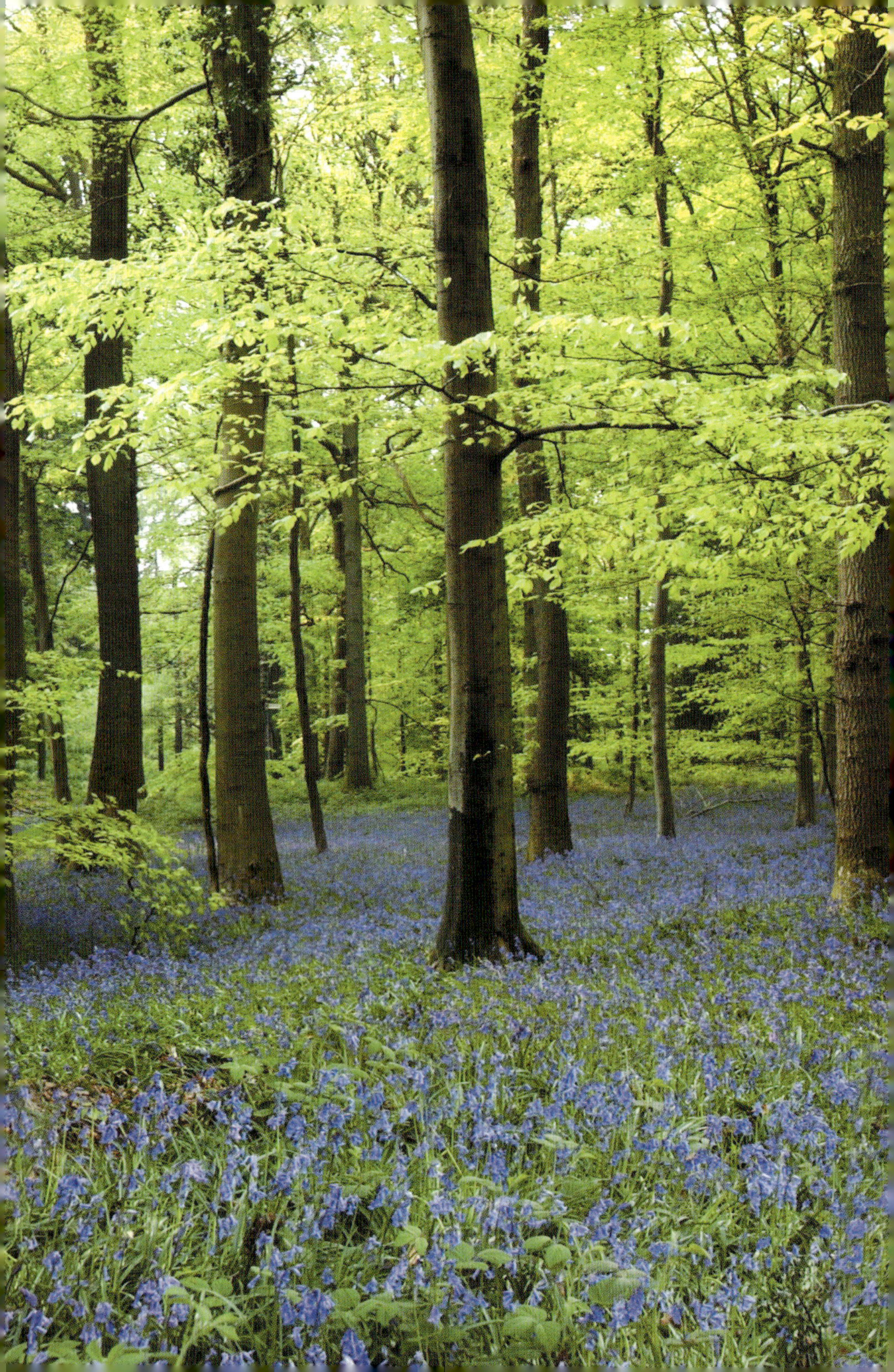

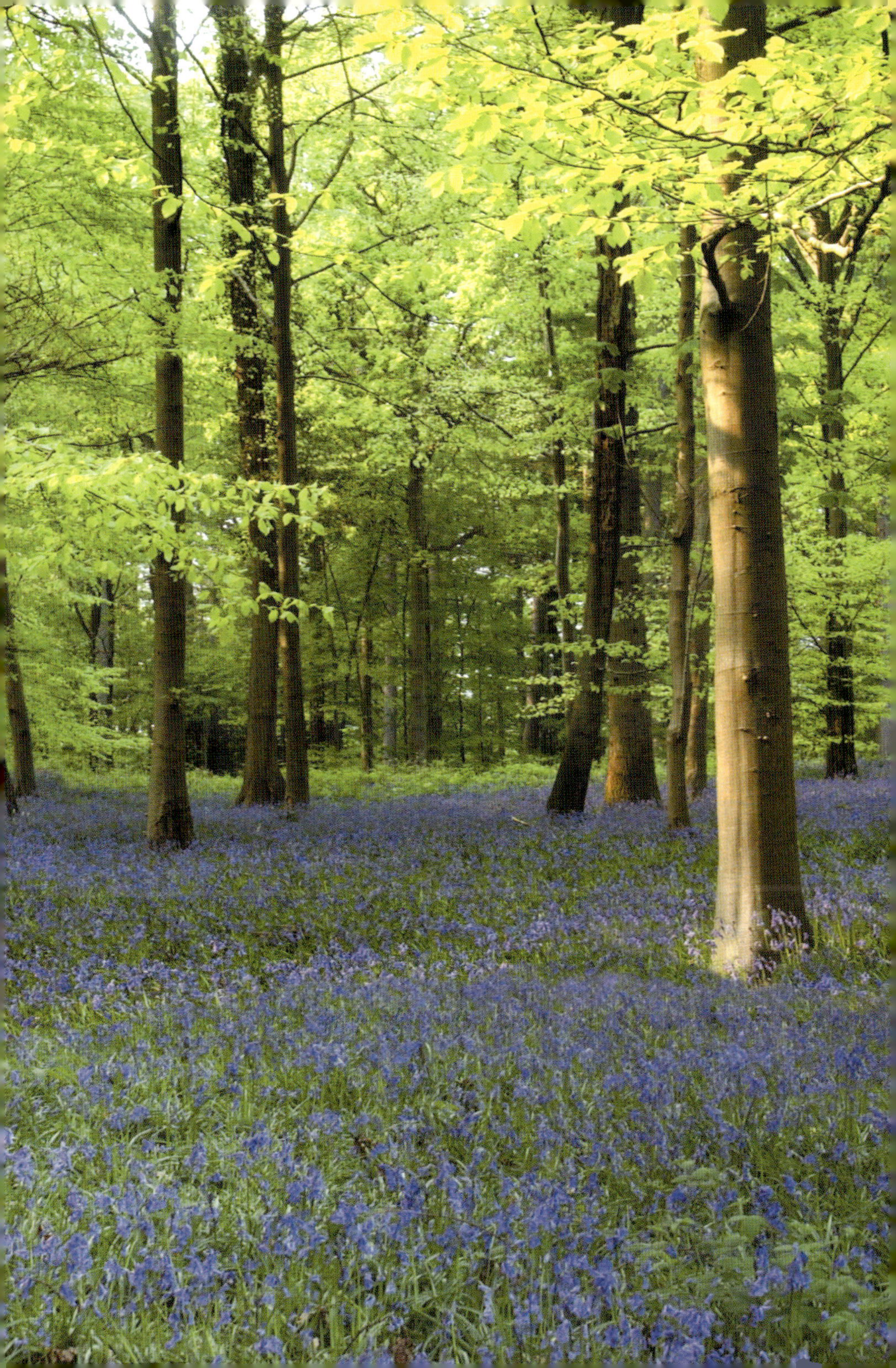

BEECHES

*Previous page: Beech trees mix with oak in Dean's
most famous bluebell wood at Bradley Hill.*

*Opposite: The roots of one of several huge beeches
in Lydney Park (see next page) are traversed by
woodman Brian Reece.*

*Below: Brian Mahony (Deputy Surveyor until
1999) chose this beech, rather than an oak, for his
named tree: Mahony beech is adjacent to the Royal
oaks by Speech House.*

**Lydney Park is open in the spring; some of the private
woodland here is crossed by footpaths.**

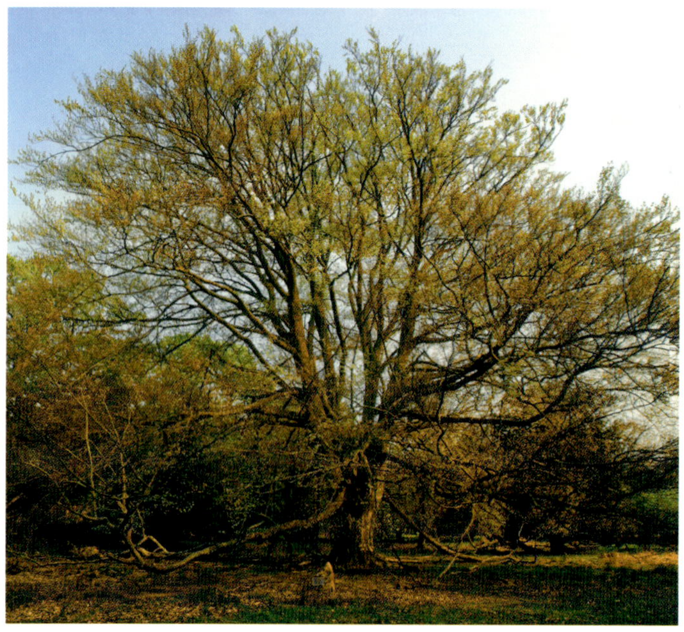

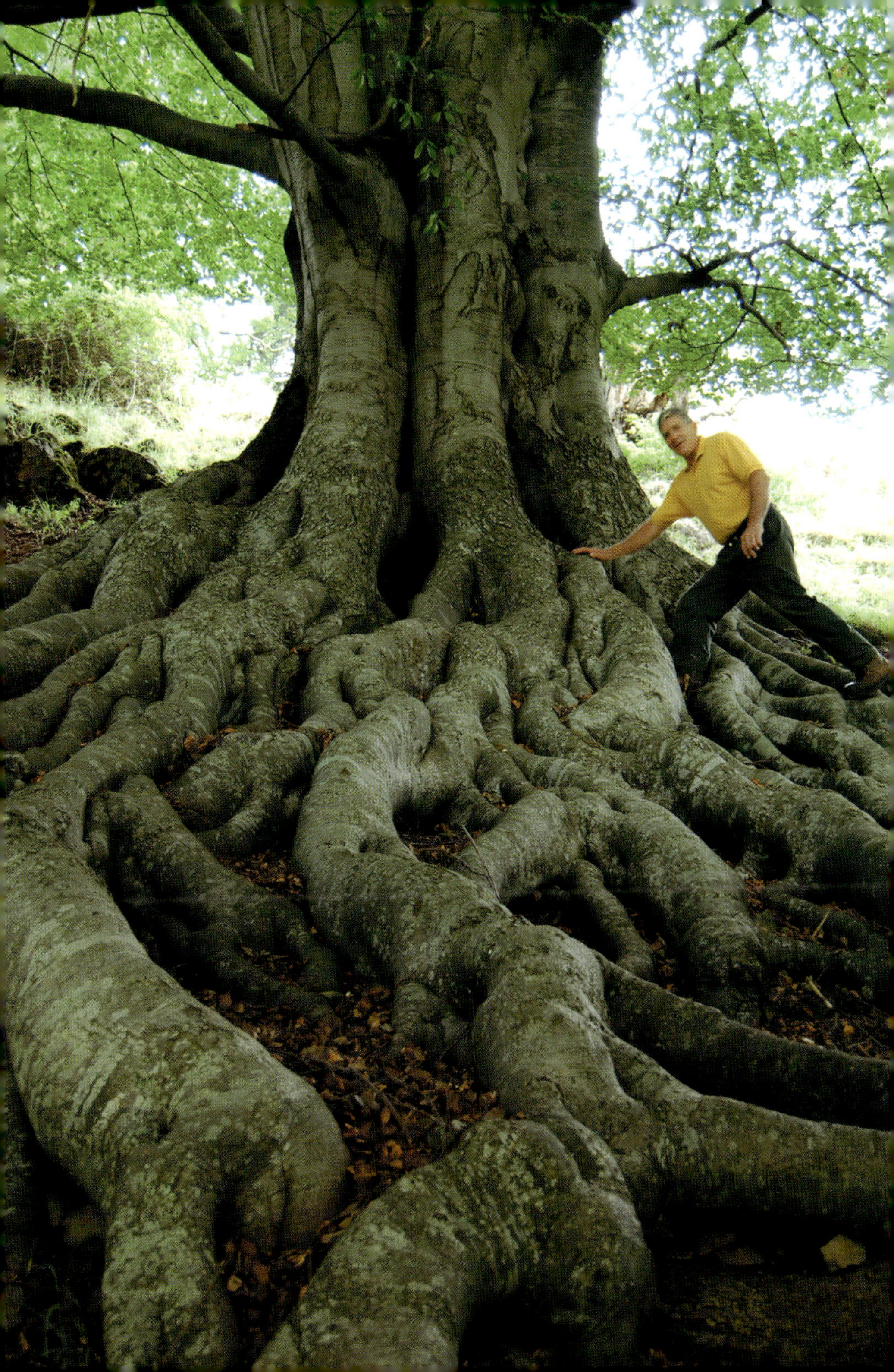

LYDNEY PARK CHAMPIONS

Opposite: Two avenues of mature plane trees grace the wide valley bottom in Lydney Park Estate. The tree shown here is claimed as the biggest in Britain – not the tallest, but the broadest of girth.

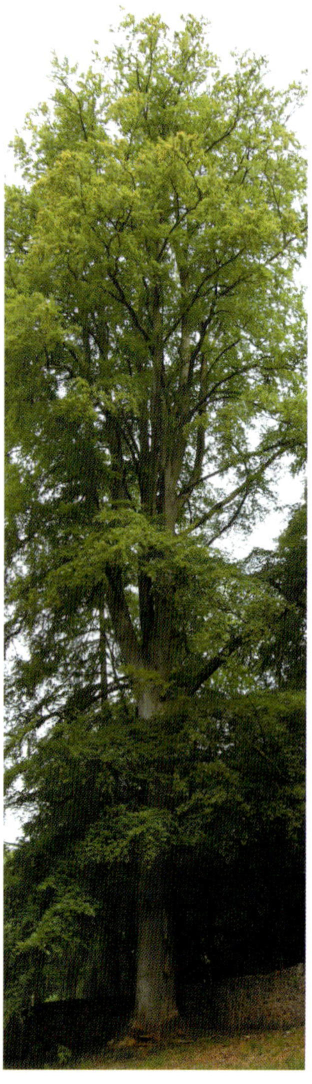

Left: Higher up the valley is another champion, the tallest beech in the country. The smooth bark of beech trees seems to attract vandals: the detail shows visitors can be more in love with their own names than of the trees they have come to see.

Lydney Park is open in the spring; some of the private woodland here is crossed by footpaths.

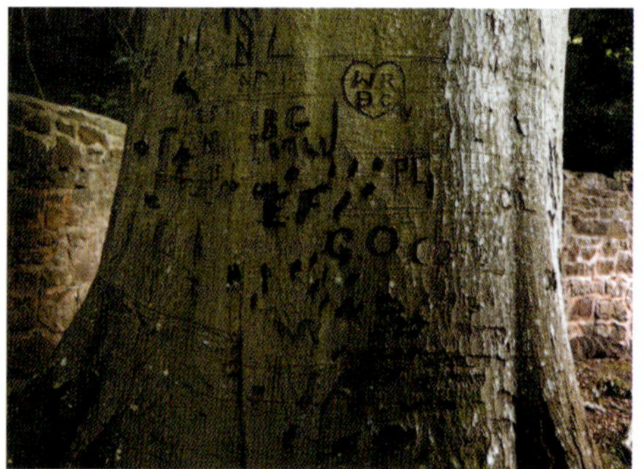

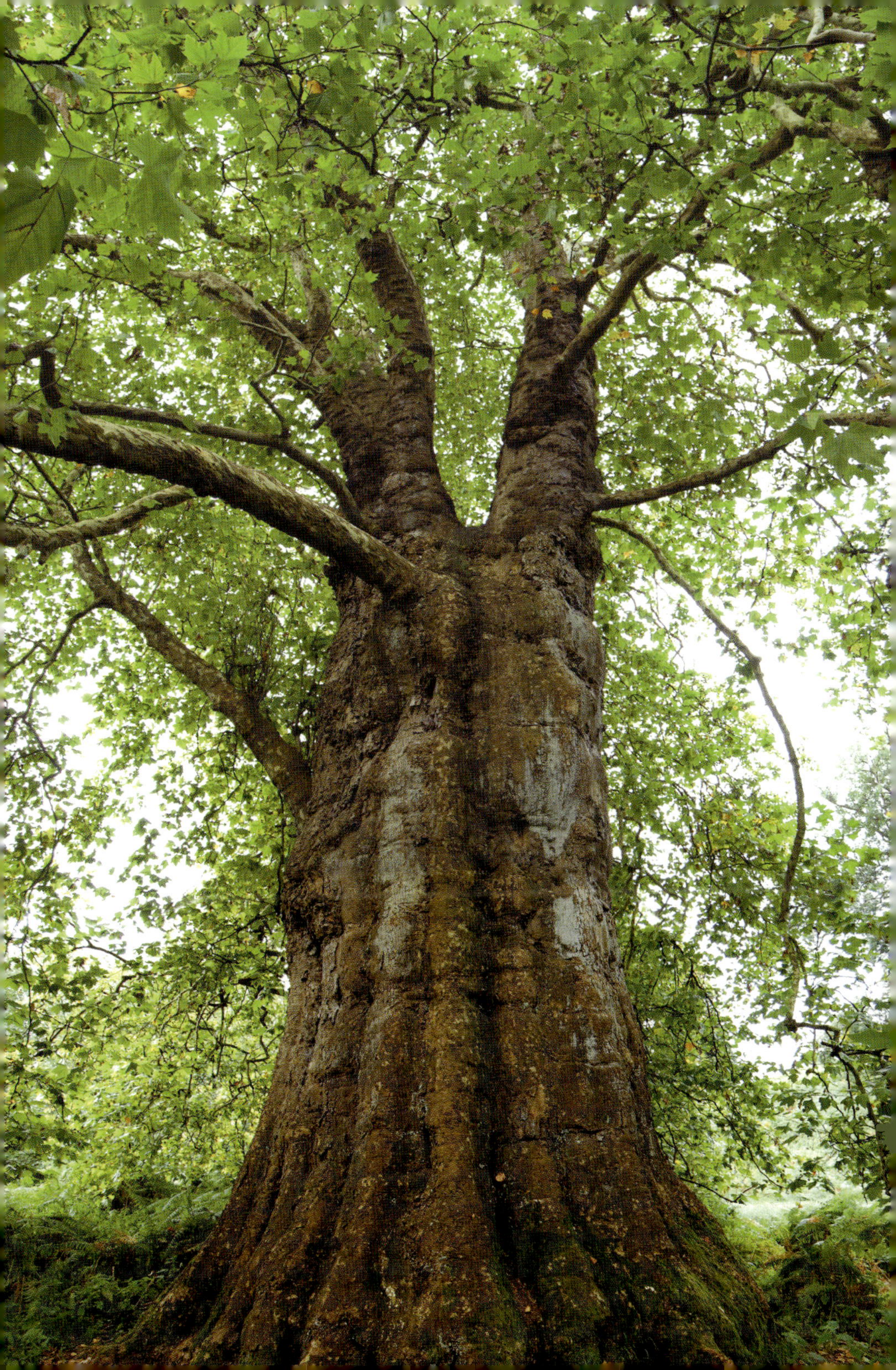

GOSLING ASH

Below: Arthur Gosling rose from trainee at Parkend Forestry School to become Director General of the Forestry Commission, and was knighted for services to forestry. Gosling ash, close to the Wye at Symonds Yat East, is the tallest deciduous tree in the Forest.

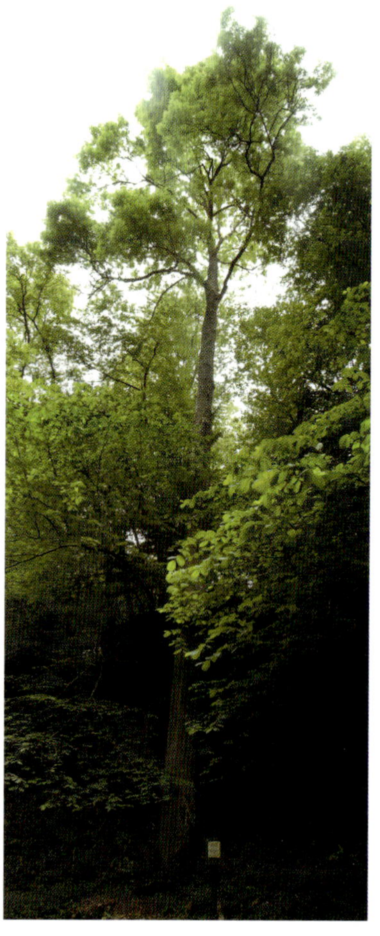

Opposite: The old woods at Oaklands contain some enormous ash boles (below, being investigated by Nick Assirati) resulting from decades of coppicing.

Oaklands Park is private but some sections are visible from public paths.

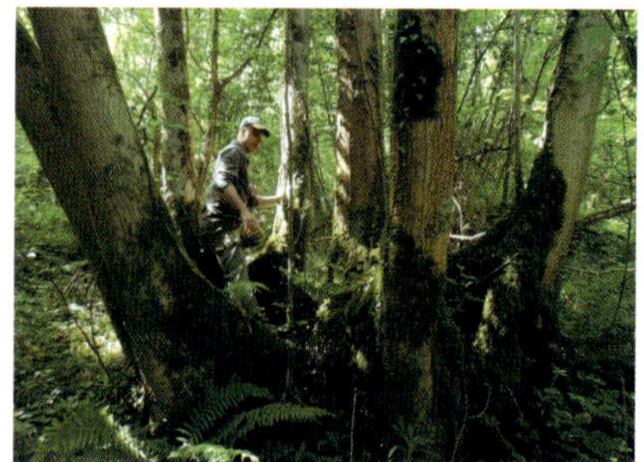

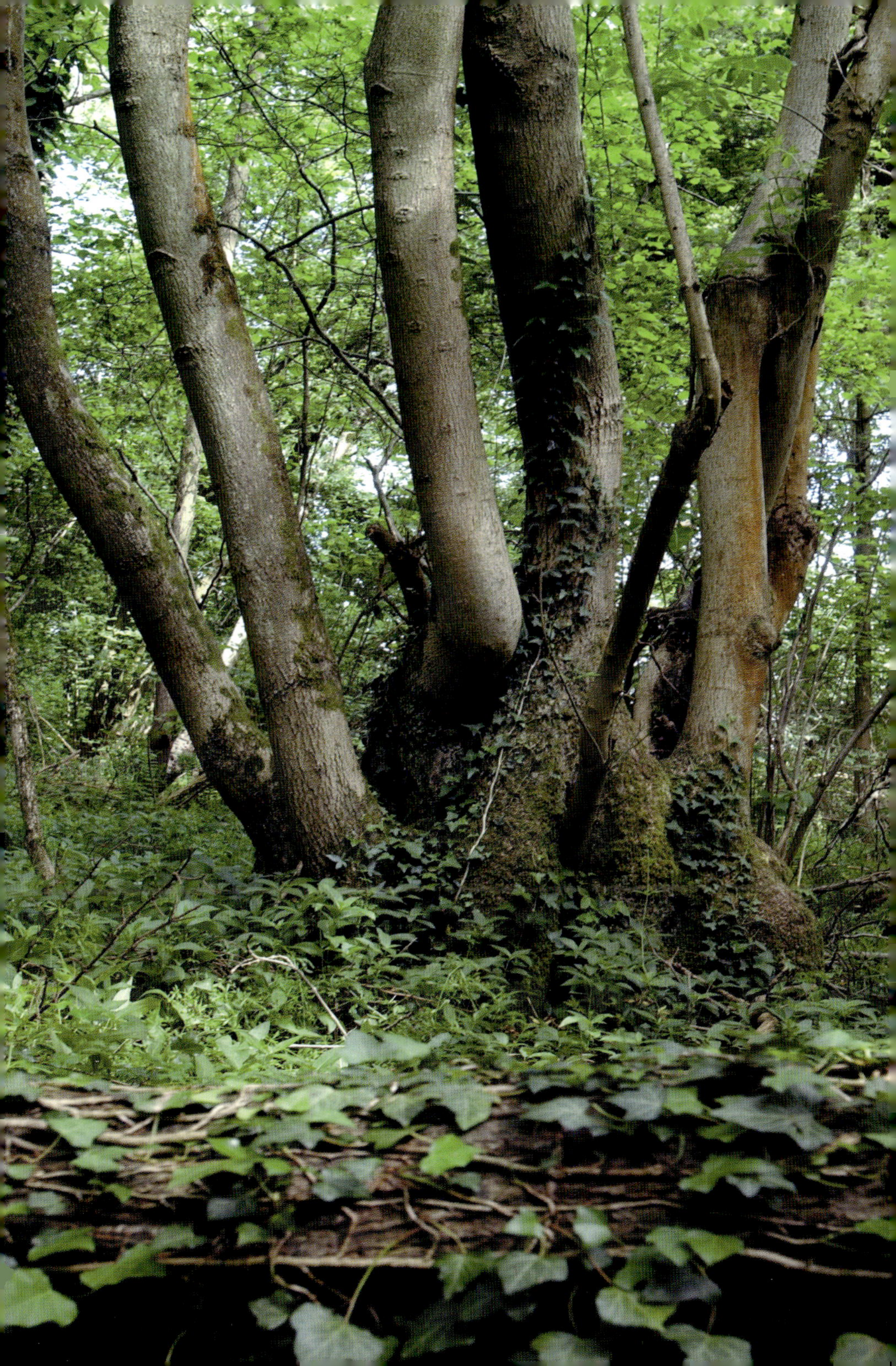

OAKLANDS WOODS

As well as the ash boles (previous page), mixed planting in the ancient oak woods (see page 34) includes a Scots pine (opposite) and a pair of elms framing a sequoia (below).

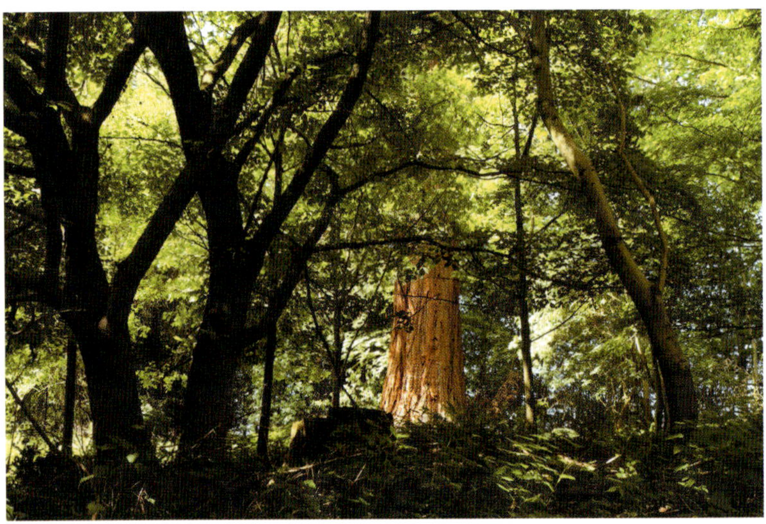

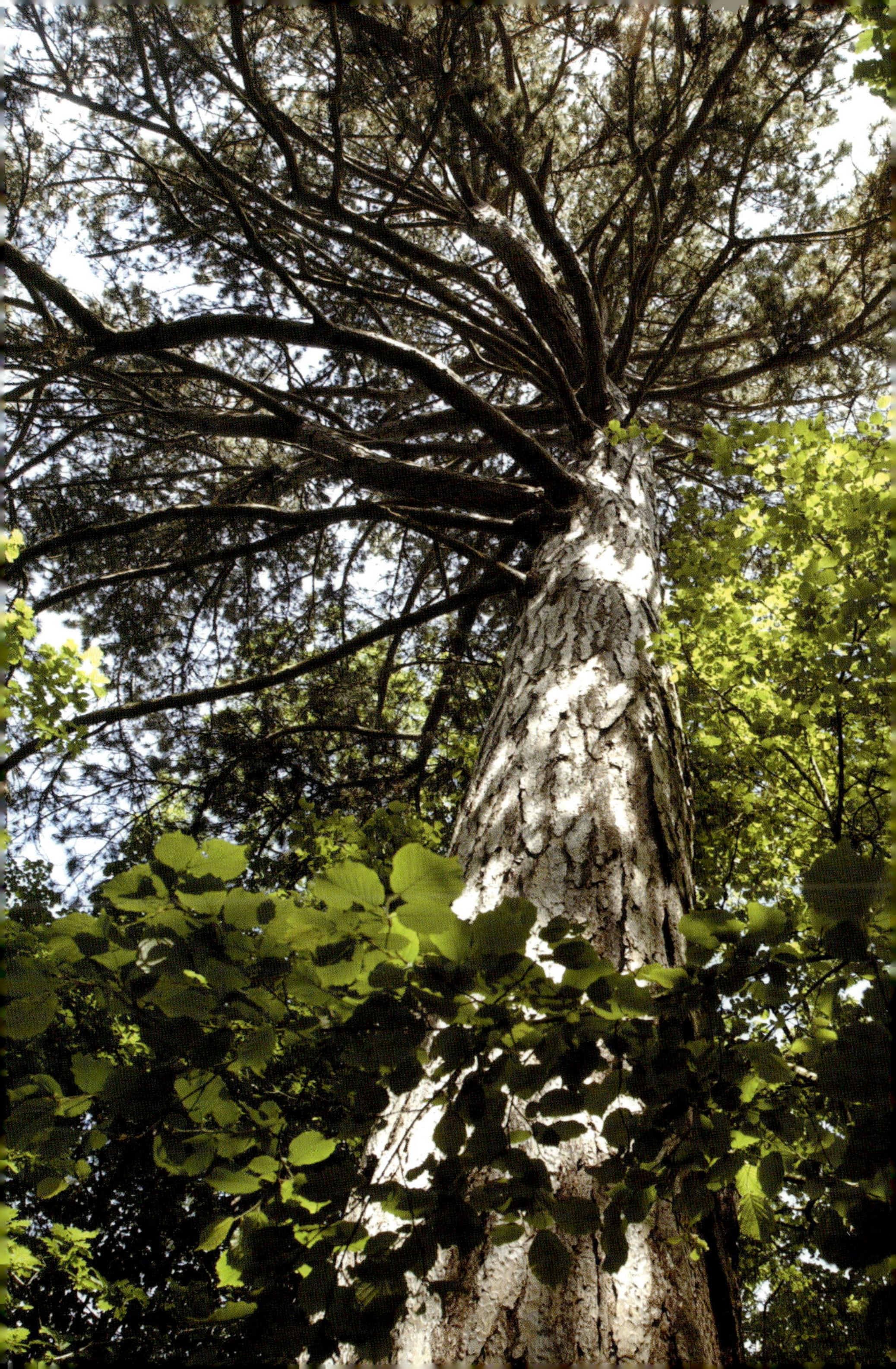

LIMES

*Both our examples
are of lime avenues:
on the green at Parkend,
a commemorative avenue
for Edward VII (opposite
and right), and on the
Speech House road just
south of New Fancy
(below). The latter is part
of an avenue that is
reputed to run from the
vicarage at Parkend to
Ruspidge.*

**628093 (Parkend); 614079
(Speech House road). See map
on page 72.**

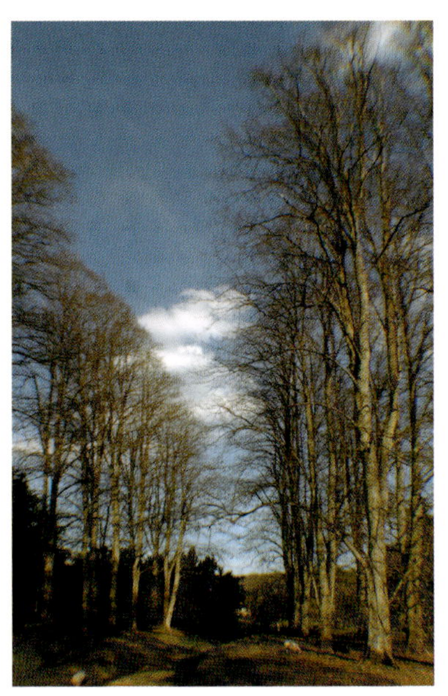

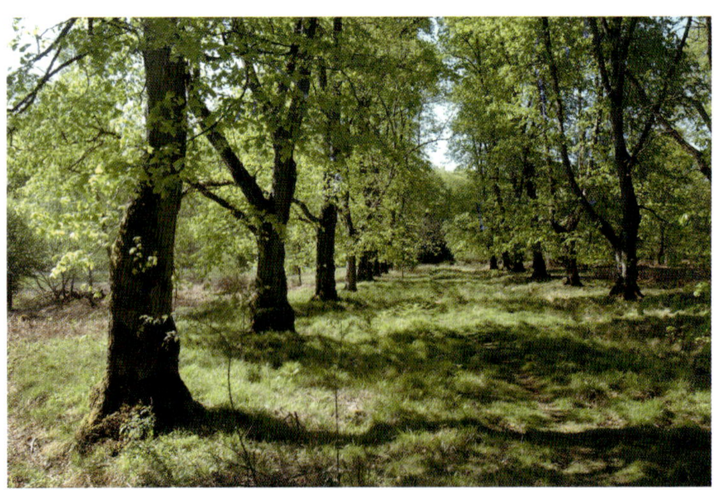

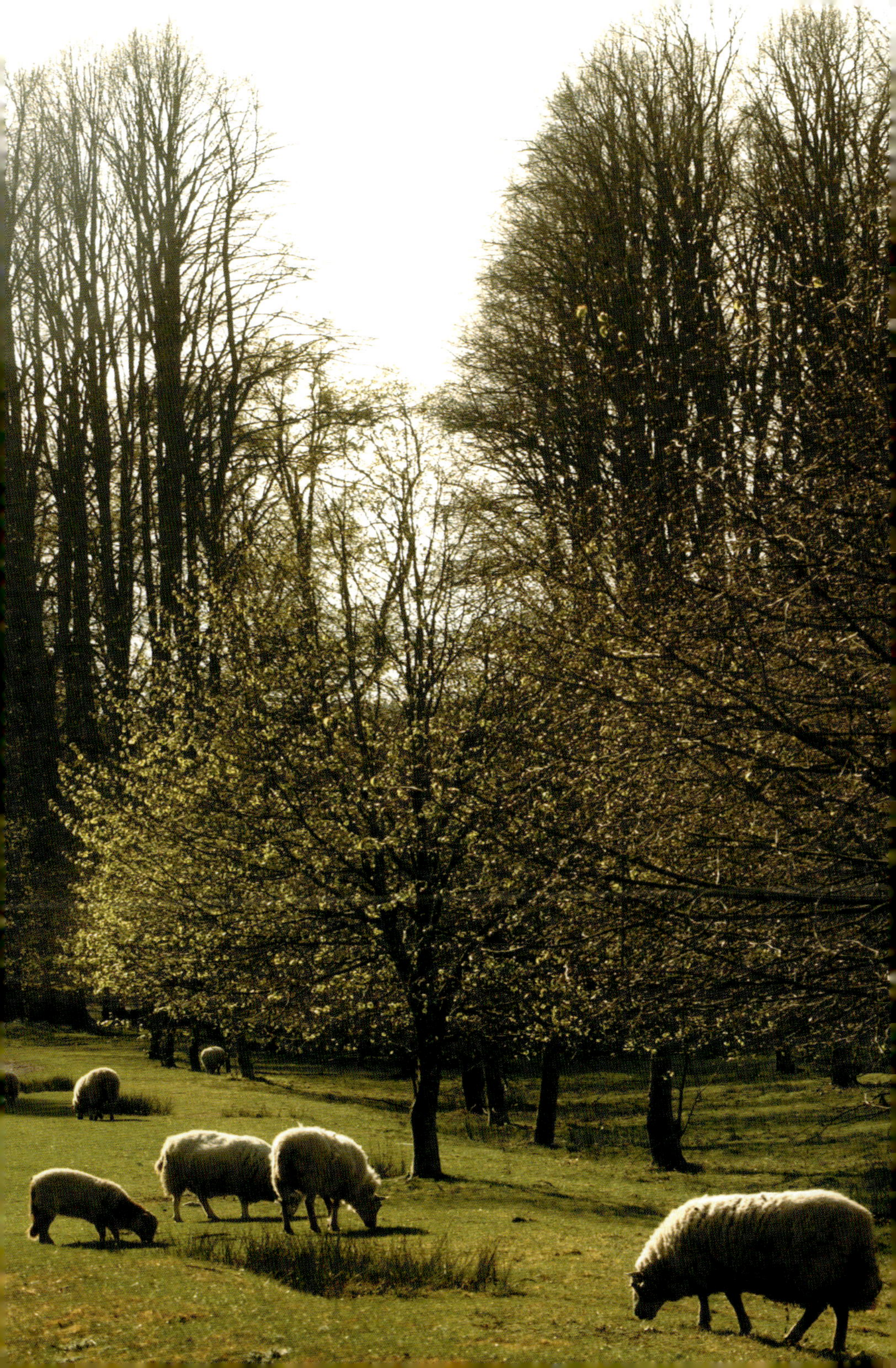

HORSE CHESTNUTS

Another avenue, this time of chestnuts, on the Bream road towards Devil's Chapel. Chestnut 'candles' are a very distinctive flower for a tree and the nuts provide schoolboys with conkers.

589058

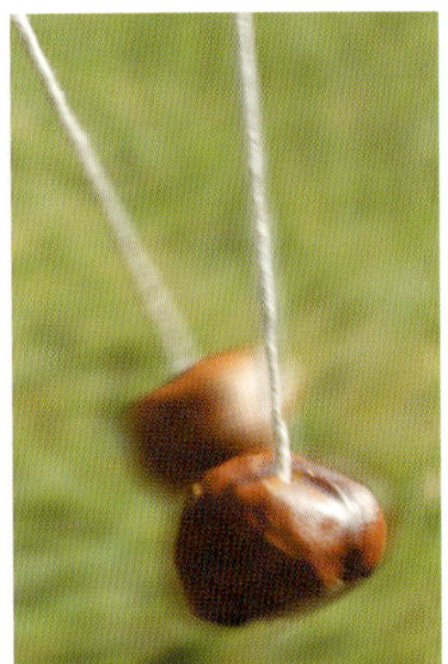
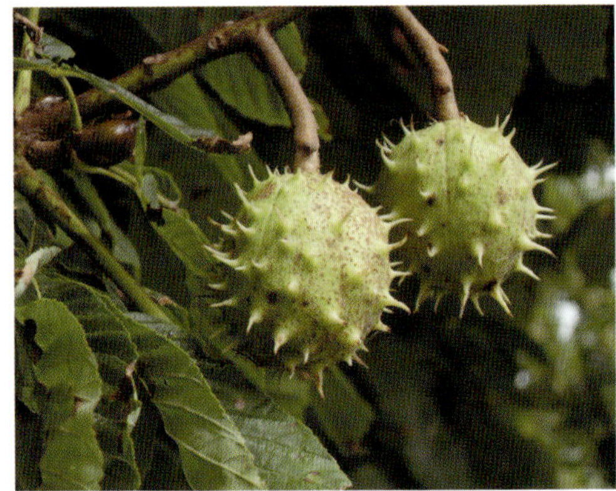
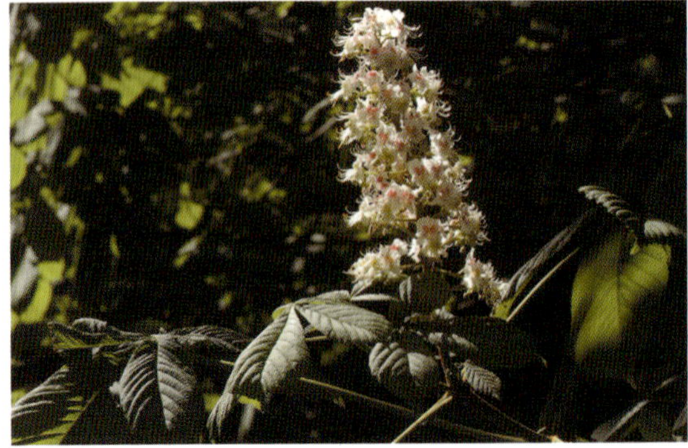

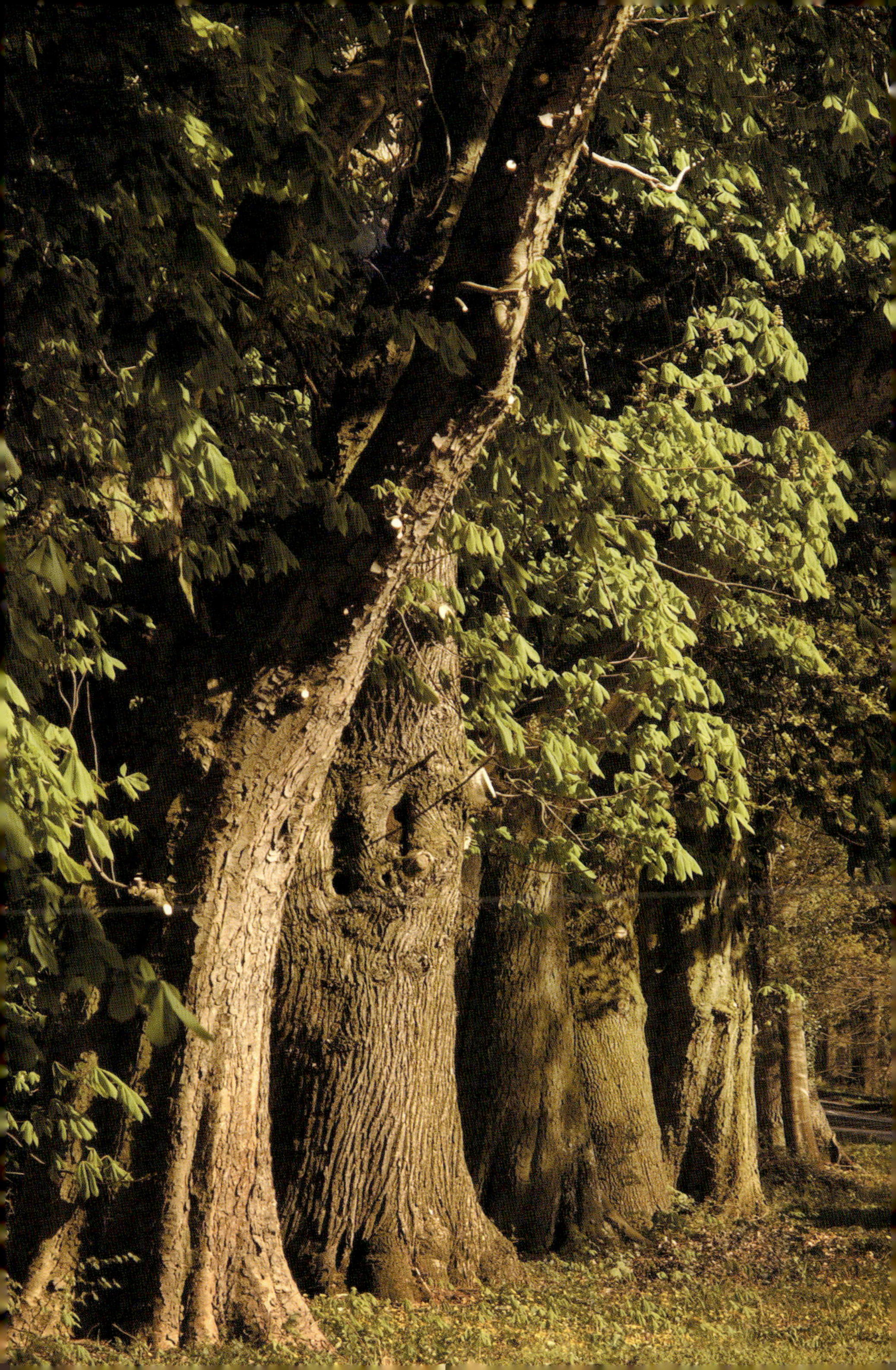

SWEET CHESTNUTS

The two specimens opposite, noticeably slow into leaf compared with the surrounding oaks, are near Beechenhurst Lodge on the Sculpture Trail. The tree on the left plays host to a temporarily missing 'Melissa's Swing', part of the Dean Sculpture Trail (page 88).

Chestnuts are a rare edible fruit from Forest trees.

615122: Follow the Sculpture Trail map available from the Forest visitor centre at Beechenhurst Lodge.

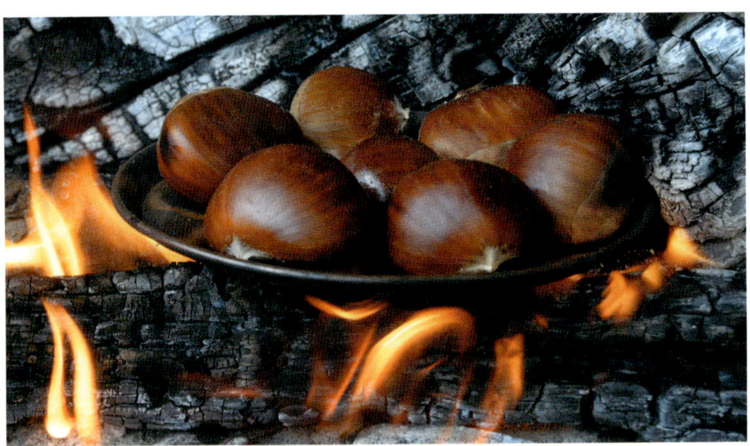

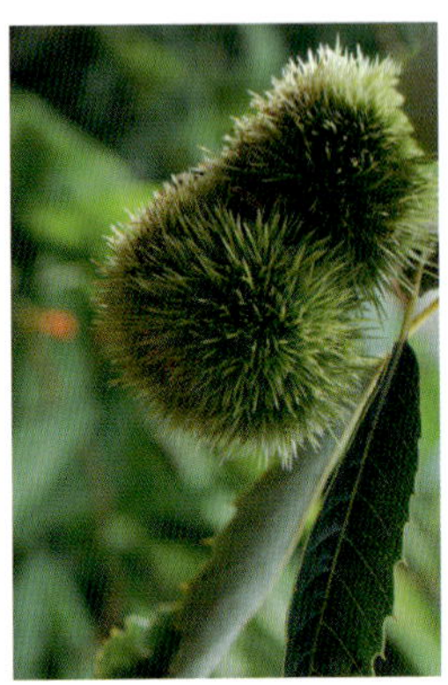

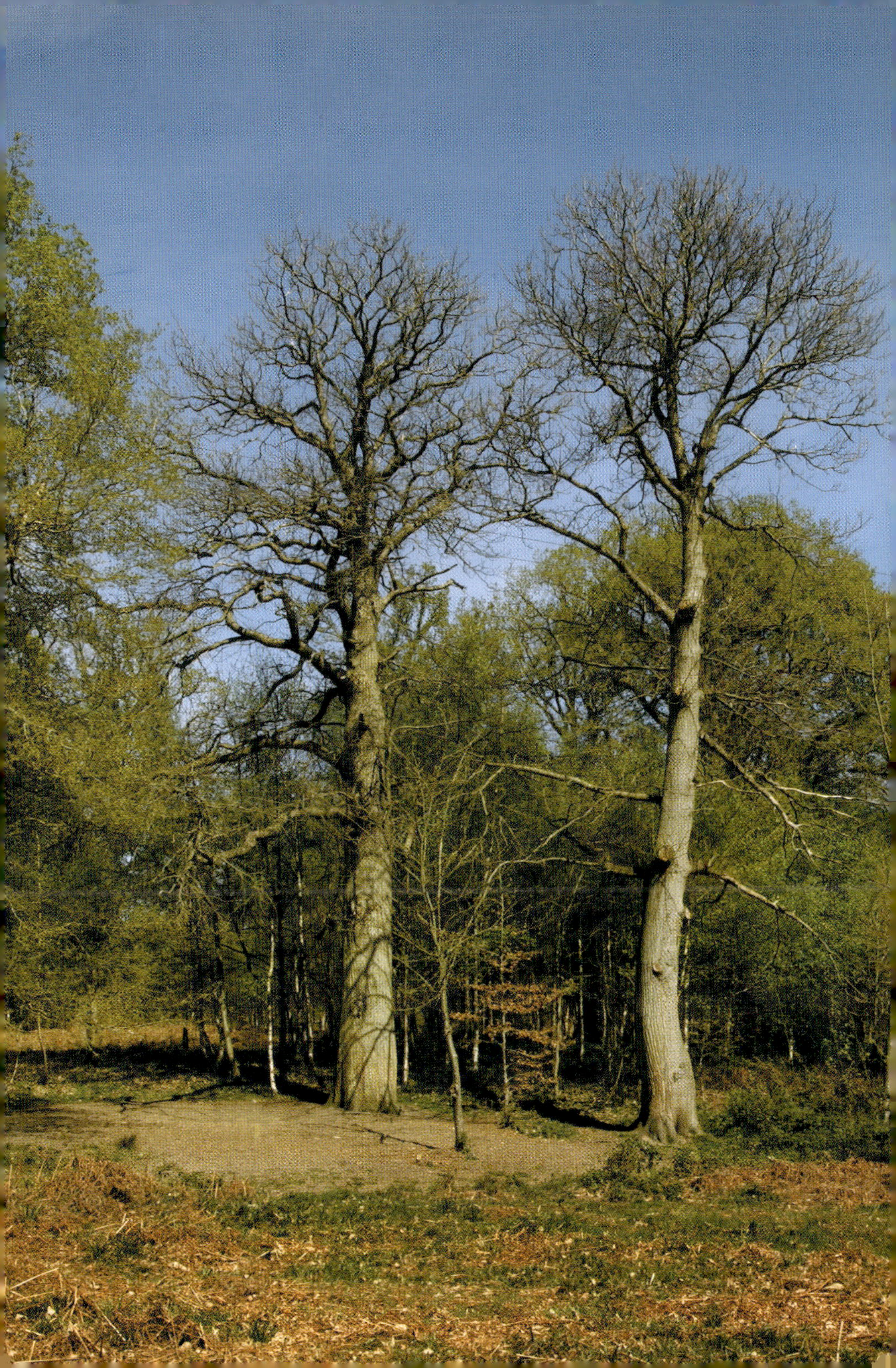

YORKLEY SYCAMORE

This variegated sycamore stands on a tiny patch of Forestry land completely surrounded by suburban housing. Legal or not, most of the nineteenth-century village development in Dean was on Forest land. Legend has it that if a squatter could build a chimney stack overnight it would legitimise his claim.

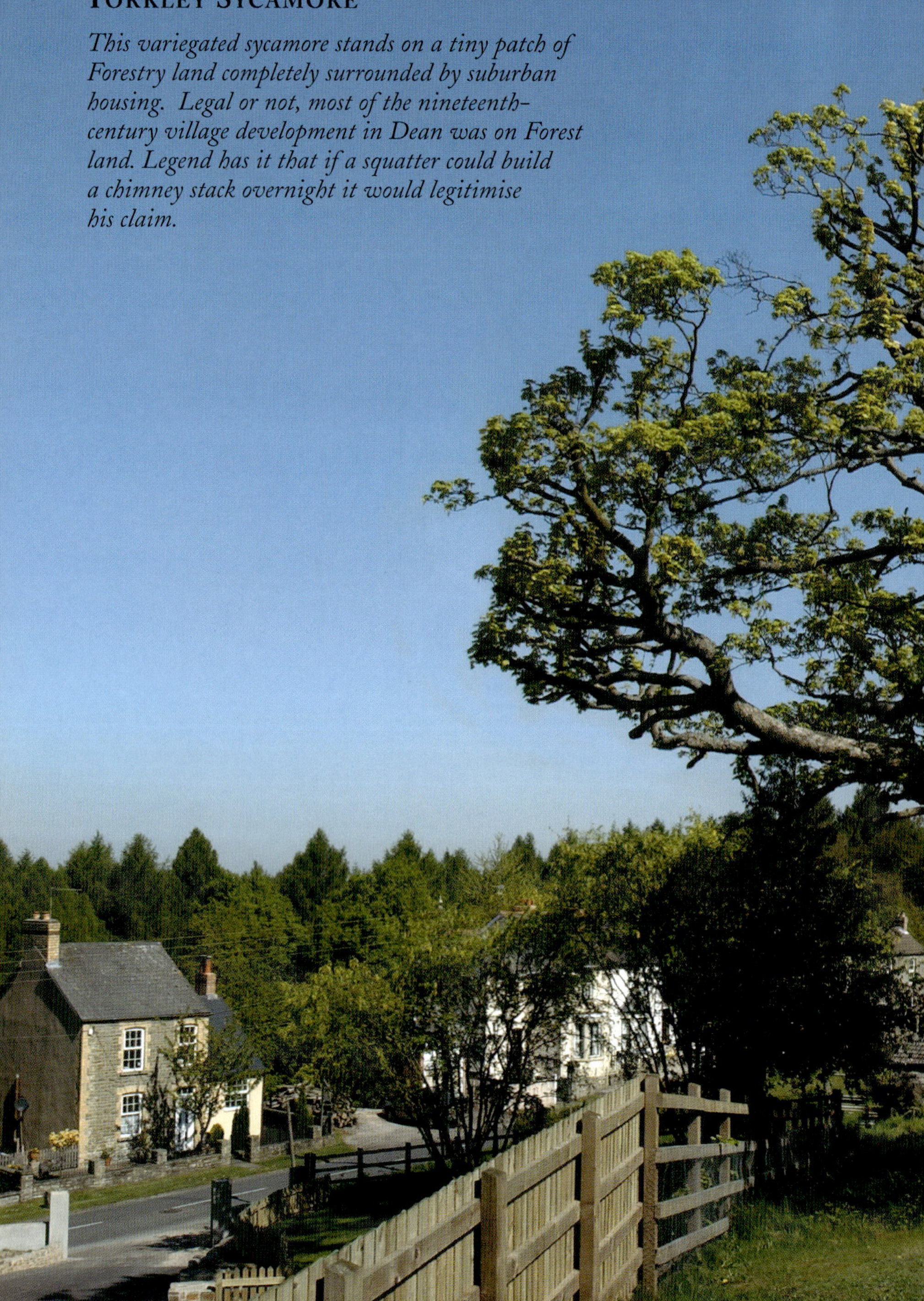

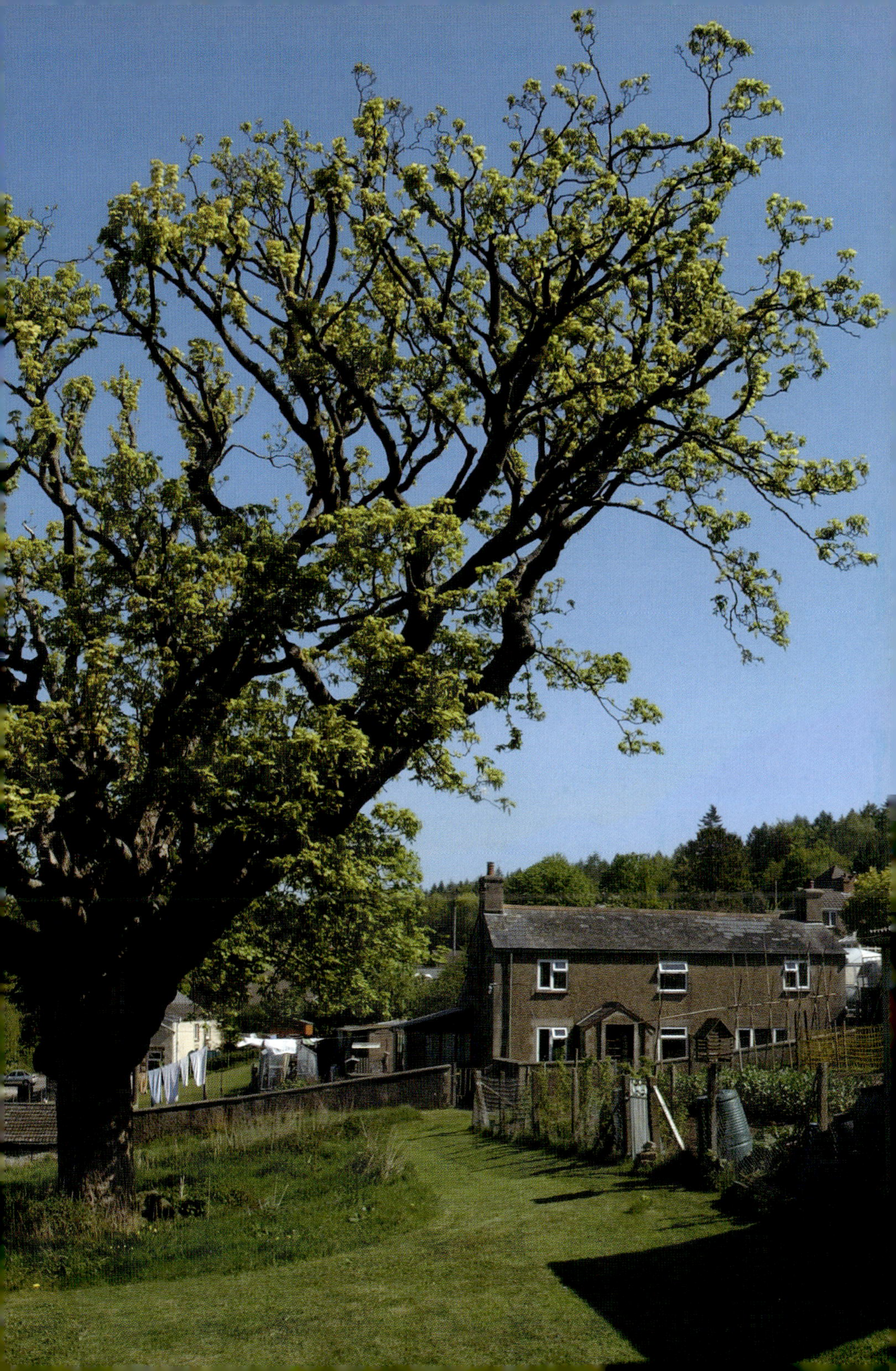

MAY HILL

May Hill is beyond the traditional limit of the Forest but is included here as it is such an iconic landmark. Its wonderful grove of Corsican pines was planted to celebrate Queen Victoria's golden jubilee.

696213

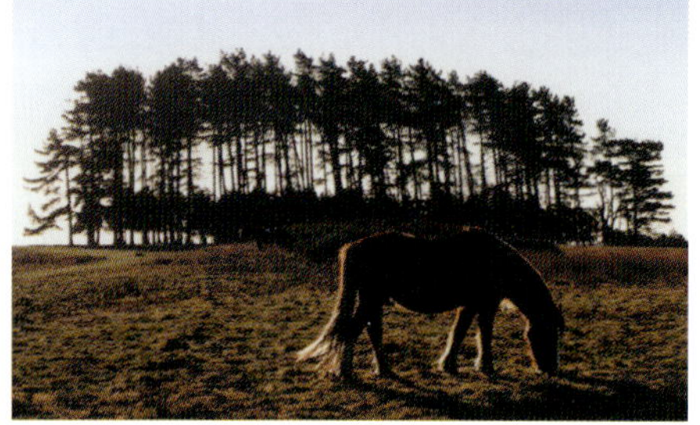

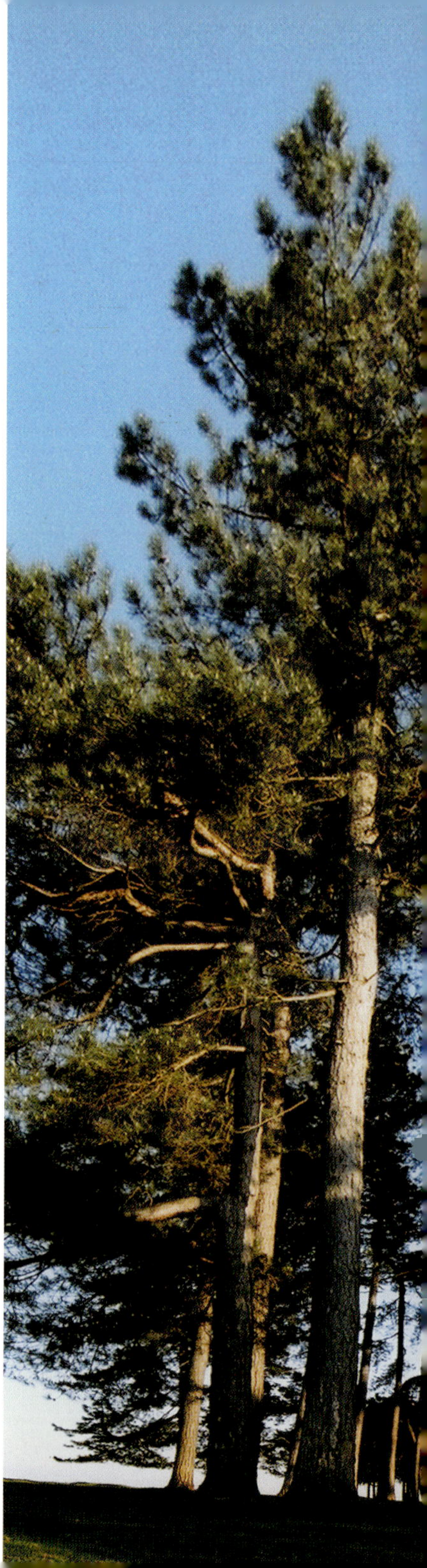

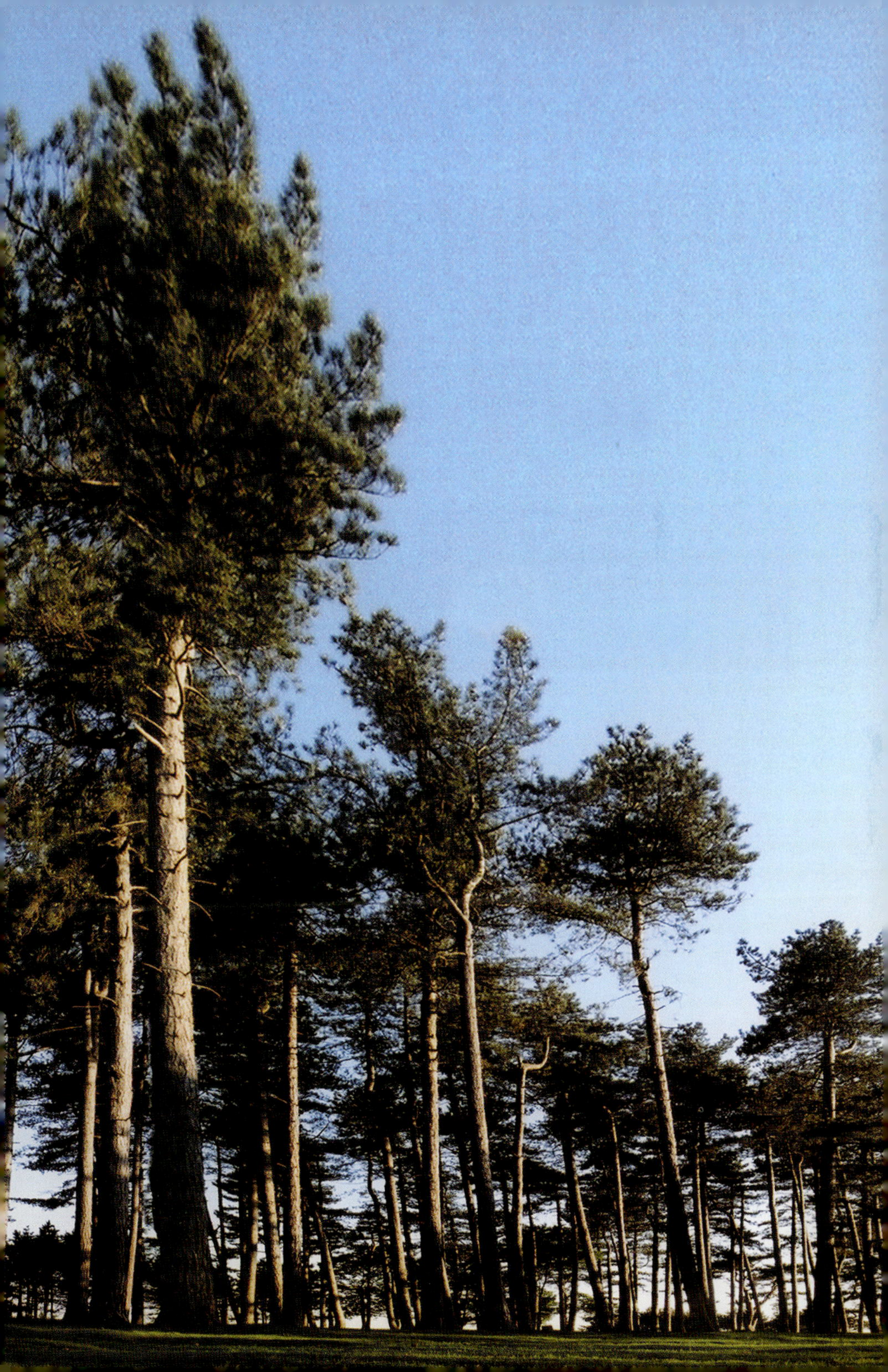

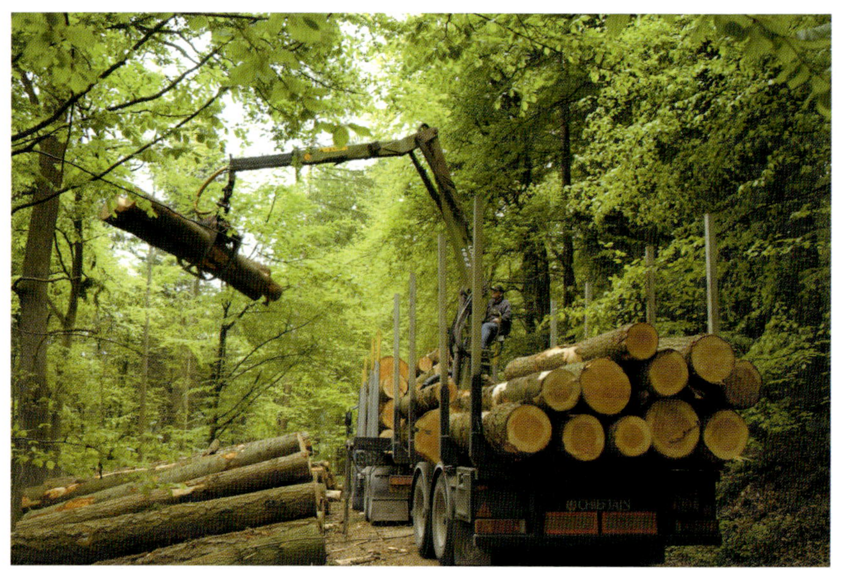

3

WOODWORK
(AND PLAY)

By far the biggest area of Dean is owned by the government and managed by the Forestry Commission. Despite this organisation's modern remit and management, its regional head is still known by the historic title of Deputy Surveyor, an honour shared only with the New Forest.

While the primary aim of Forest Enterprise, the commercial division of the Forestry Commission, is to make a profit out of growing and selling timber, its further brief includes preserving the look of the countryside and providing access to the public for walking, picnicking and other more organised leisure activities. In order for these disparate aims to mesh in and not to conflict with one another, pragmatism and careful planning are required. Birdwatchers do not share a wood with rally drivers, though forest sheep may rub shoulders with mountain bikers; tree felling usually closes off a section of forest.

Felled timber is cut under contract by operators big and small. In 2002 Forest Enterprise ran an experiment to test the market for oak 'thinnings' (trees felled to allow more space for those remaining), which had previously been used only for pulping. Furniture makers and artists were provided with timber free of charge, on condition that the resulting work would form part of a travelling exhibition. Out of this initiative Dean Forest Oak Co-operative was formed, which now runs its own sawmill at Parkend.

Forest Planning

Seen here measuring the Verderers' oak (see page 10), Ben Lennon is Planning and Conservation Manager for the Forestry Commission in the Forest of Dean. Ben's job is to oversee the planning and management strategies for the Dean woodlands. He is also responsible for deciding which areas are to be thinned or clear-felled and which species are to be replanted.

At the heart of a traditional business, Ben uses the latest software to assist in forward planning and monitoring across his huge domain (see map below).

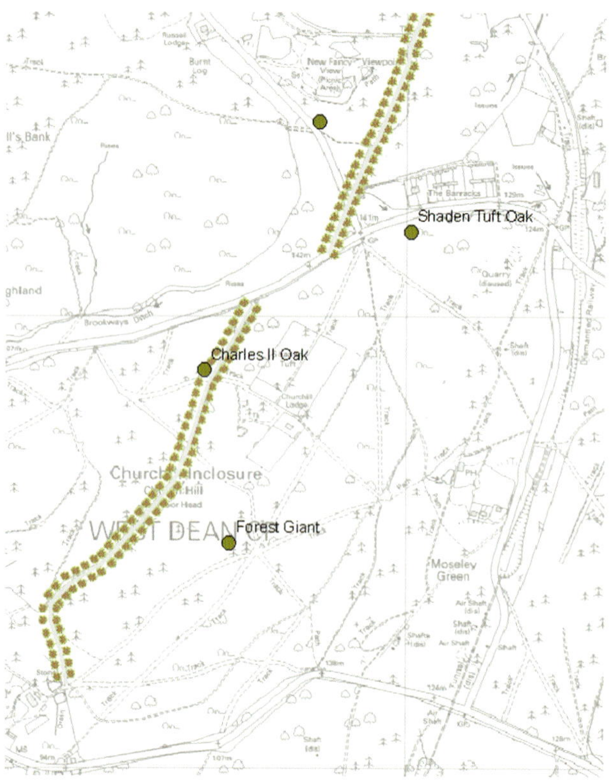

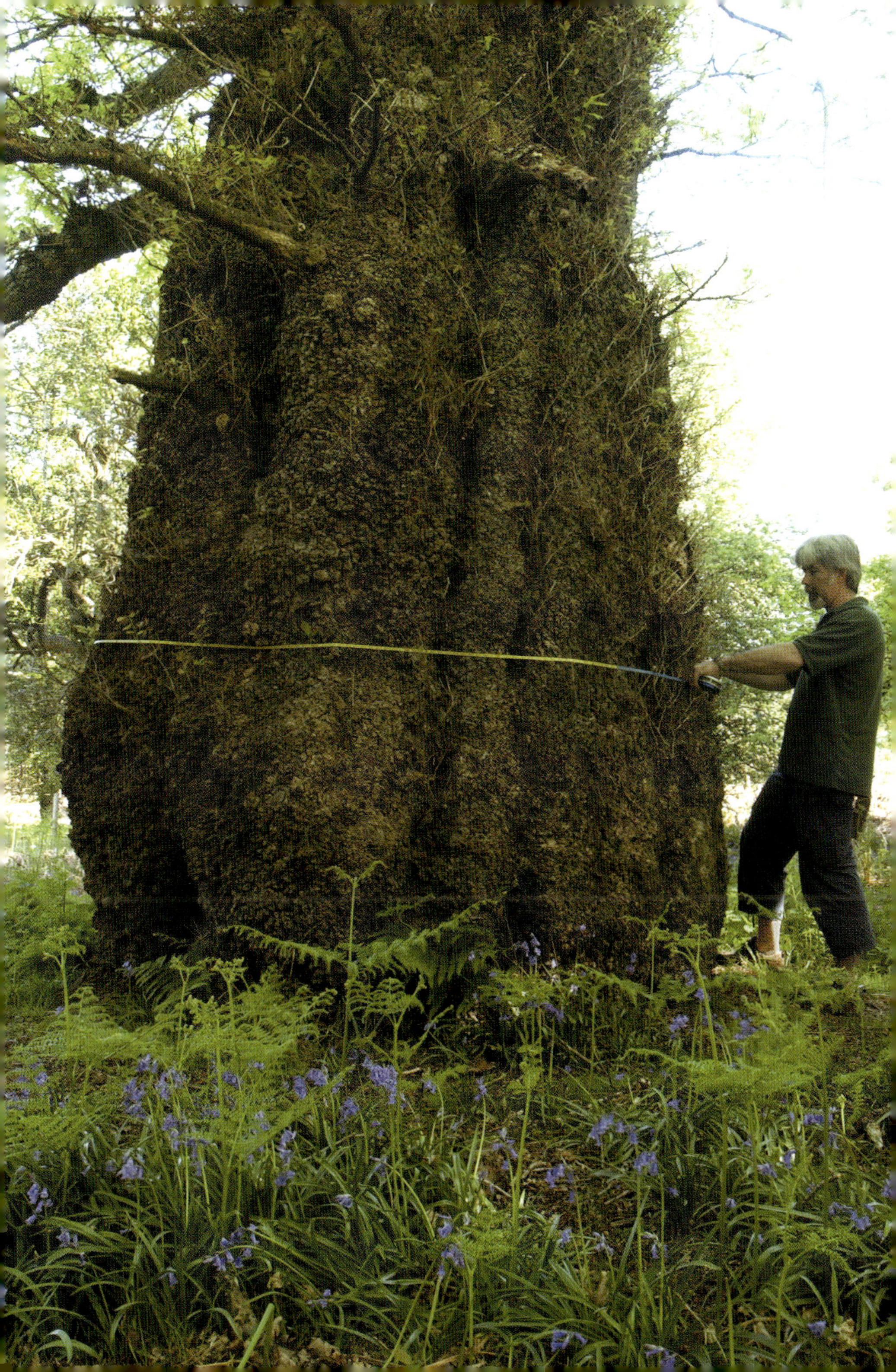

OAKLANDS REGENERATION

Opposite: Forester Nick Assirati inspects his oak seedlings.

Below: In a clearing decorated with foxgloves, with an old oak as backdrop, saplings grow up protected inside polythene tubes.

Oaklands Park is private but some sections are visible from public paths.

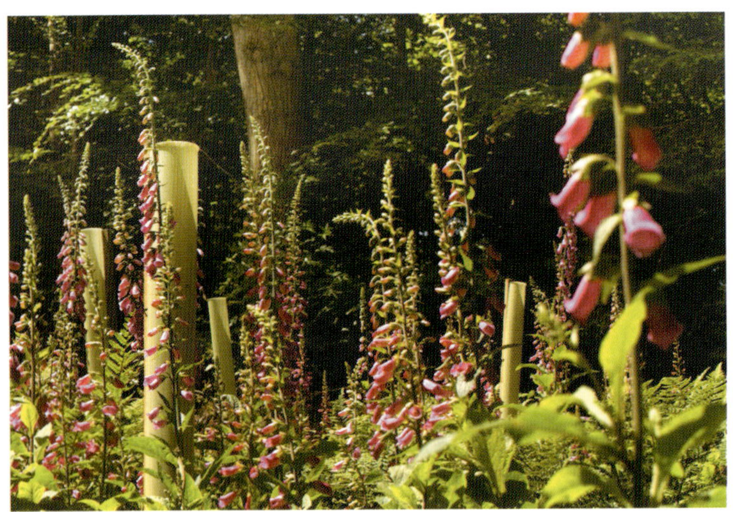

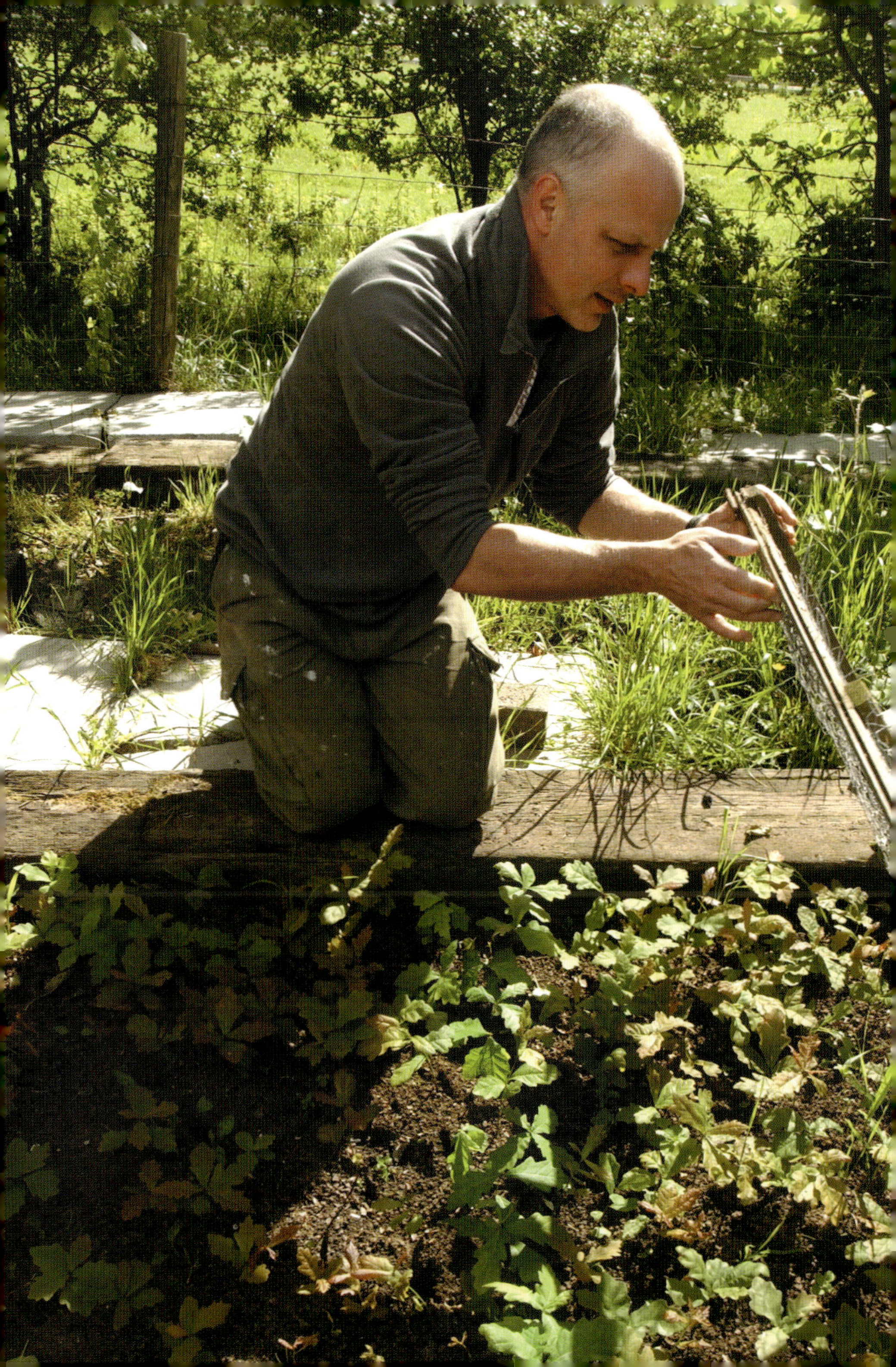

LYDNEY PARK ESTATE

Woodman Brian Reece shows off his favourite tree, a twisted sweet chestnut. As well as a champion plane tree, the park is home to several huge beeches (see pages 44 and 56). In the woods on the estate oak regeneration is taking place naturally: when the Douglas firs planted around mature oaks are felled, oak saplings will flourish in the newly brightened space.

Lydney Park is open in the spring; some of the private woodland is traversed by footpaths.

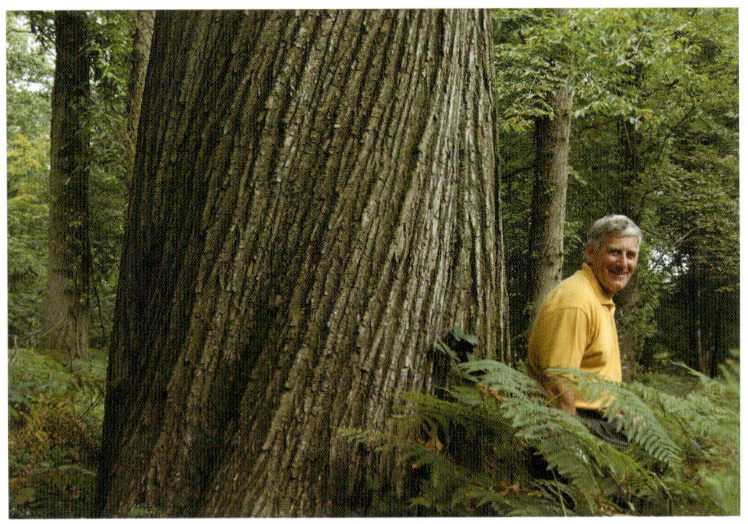

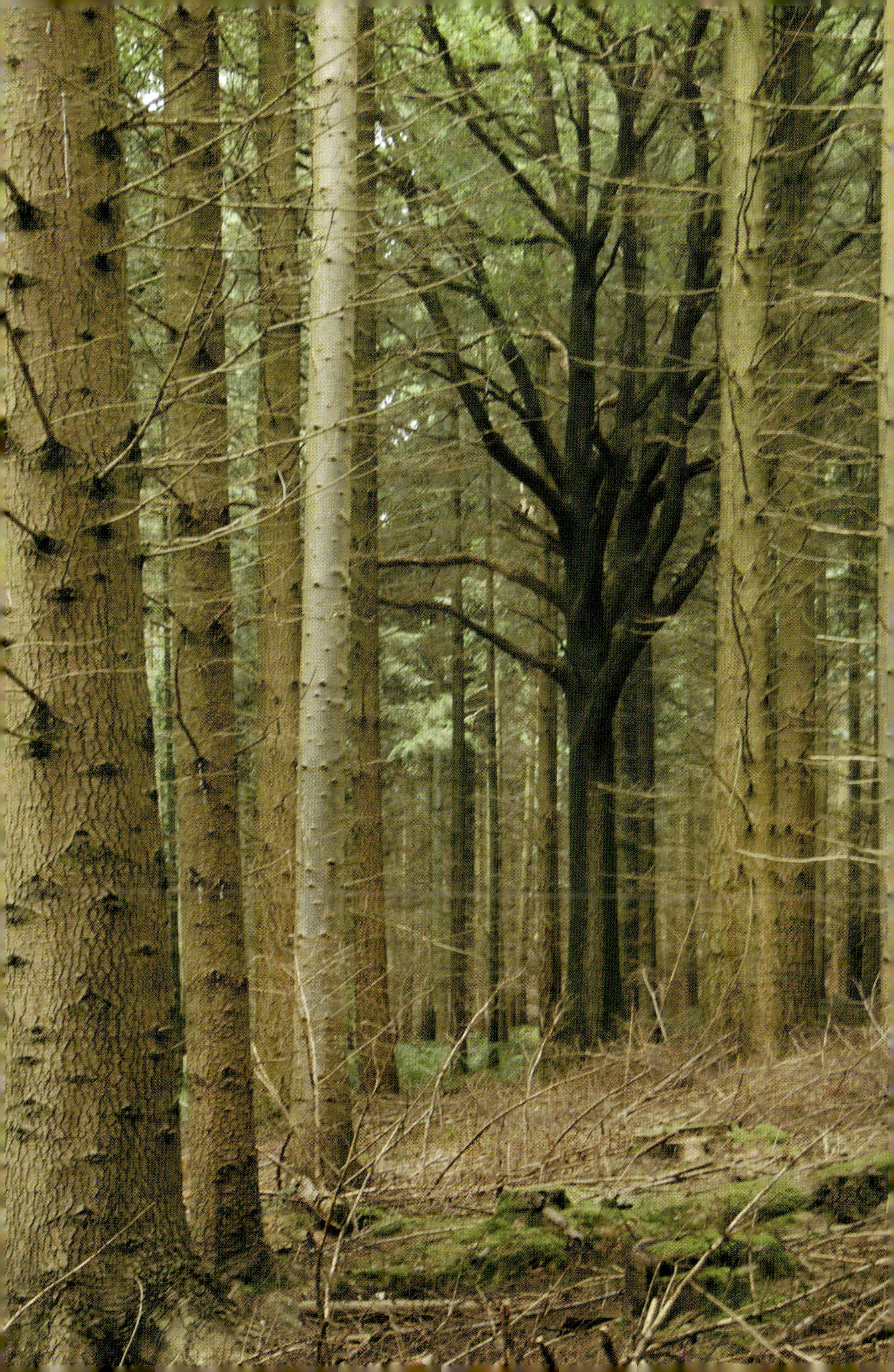

FELLING

*Ted Merrett and his son Daniel, photographed
while felling oaks in a wood at Moseley Green*

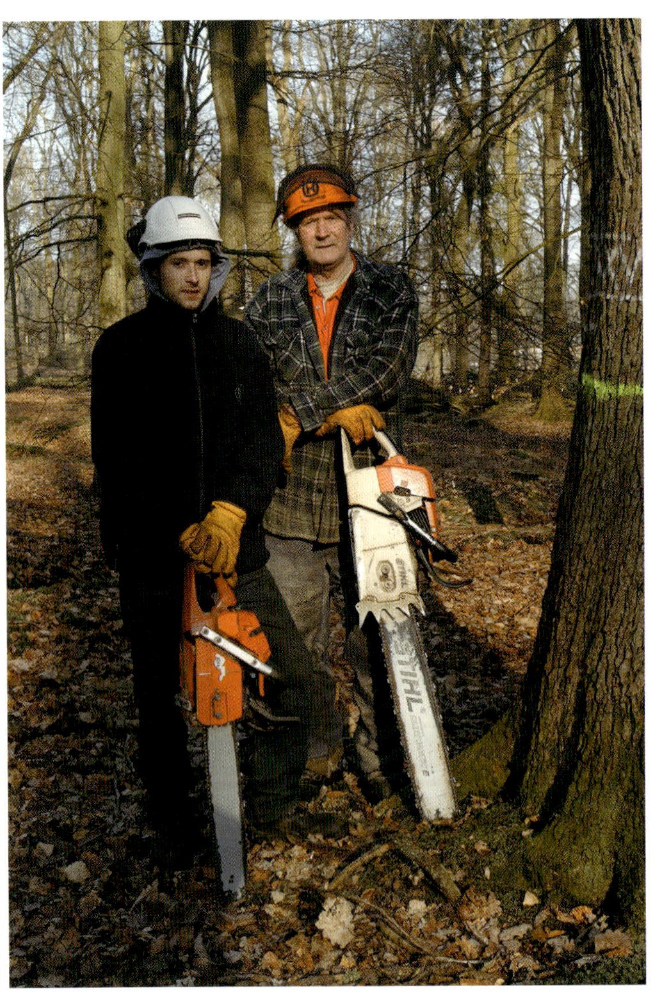

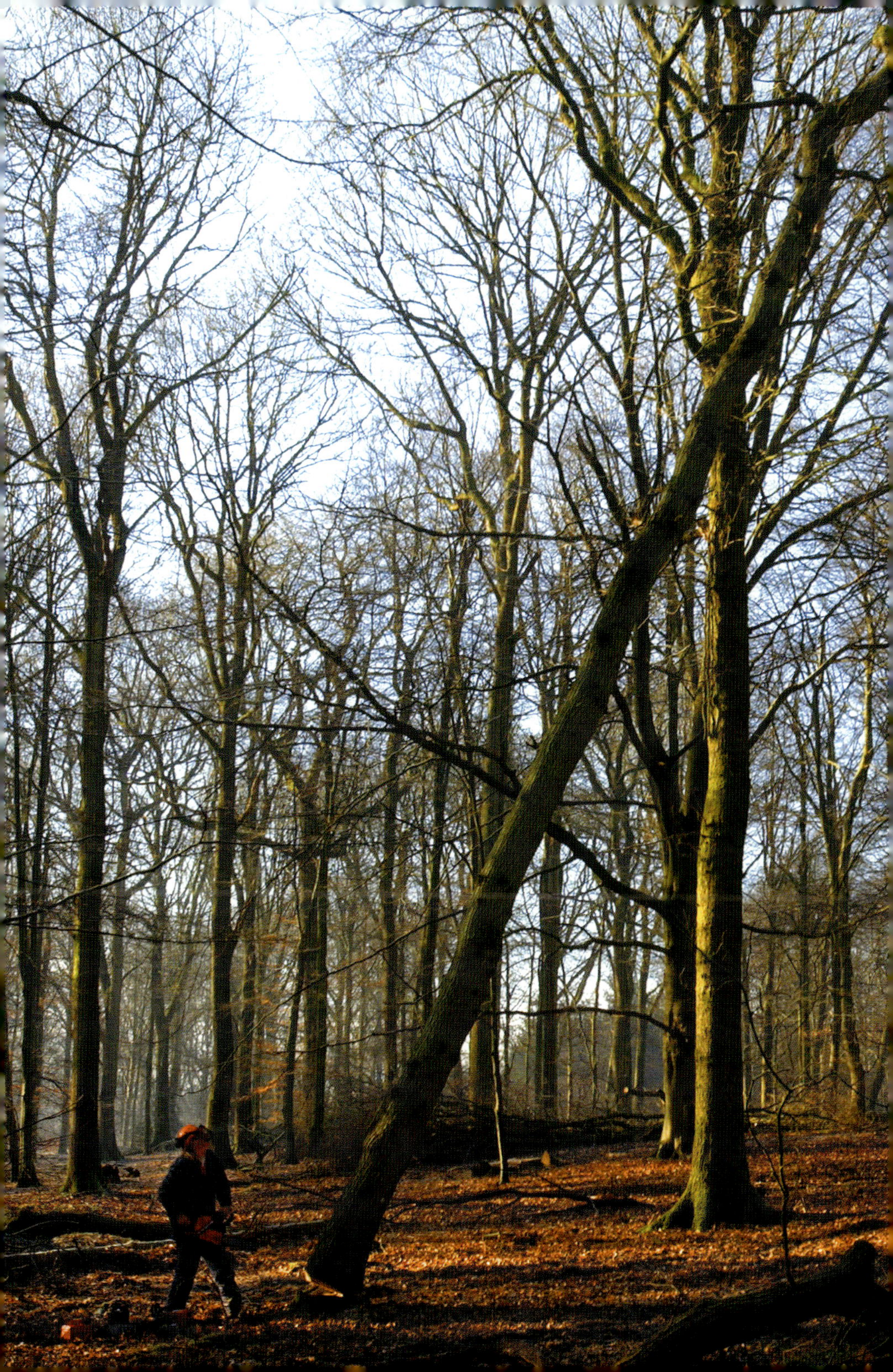

MILLING

The Dean Oak Co-operative sprang from a Forest Enterprise initiative in 2002 to find better uses for 'thinned' oak. The Co-op is supported by a company run by Chris Lewis and Tim Orson (below), here assisted by Tracey Dixon, milling at their Parkend HQ.

The Lydney Park Estate sawmill is run by Steve Harrison, assisted during university vacations by his son Scott (opposite). The bandsaws used have teeth tipped with tungsten carbide (below right).

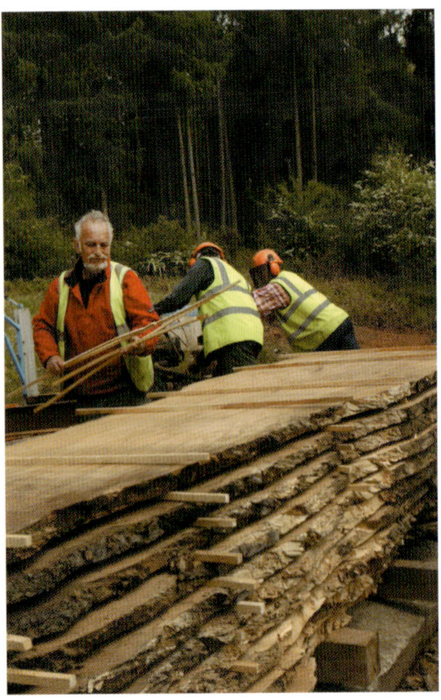

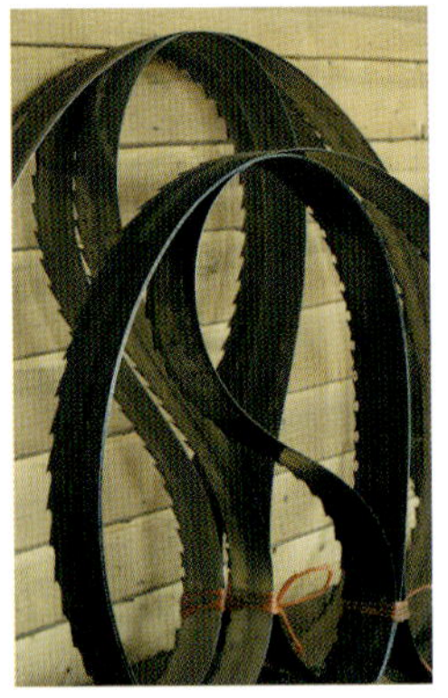

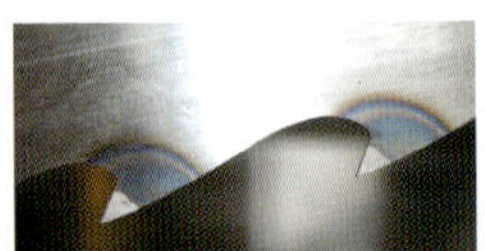

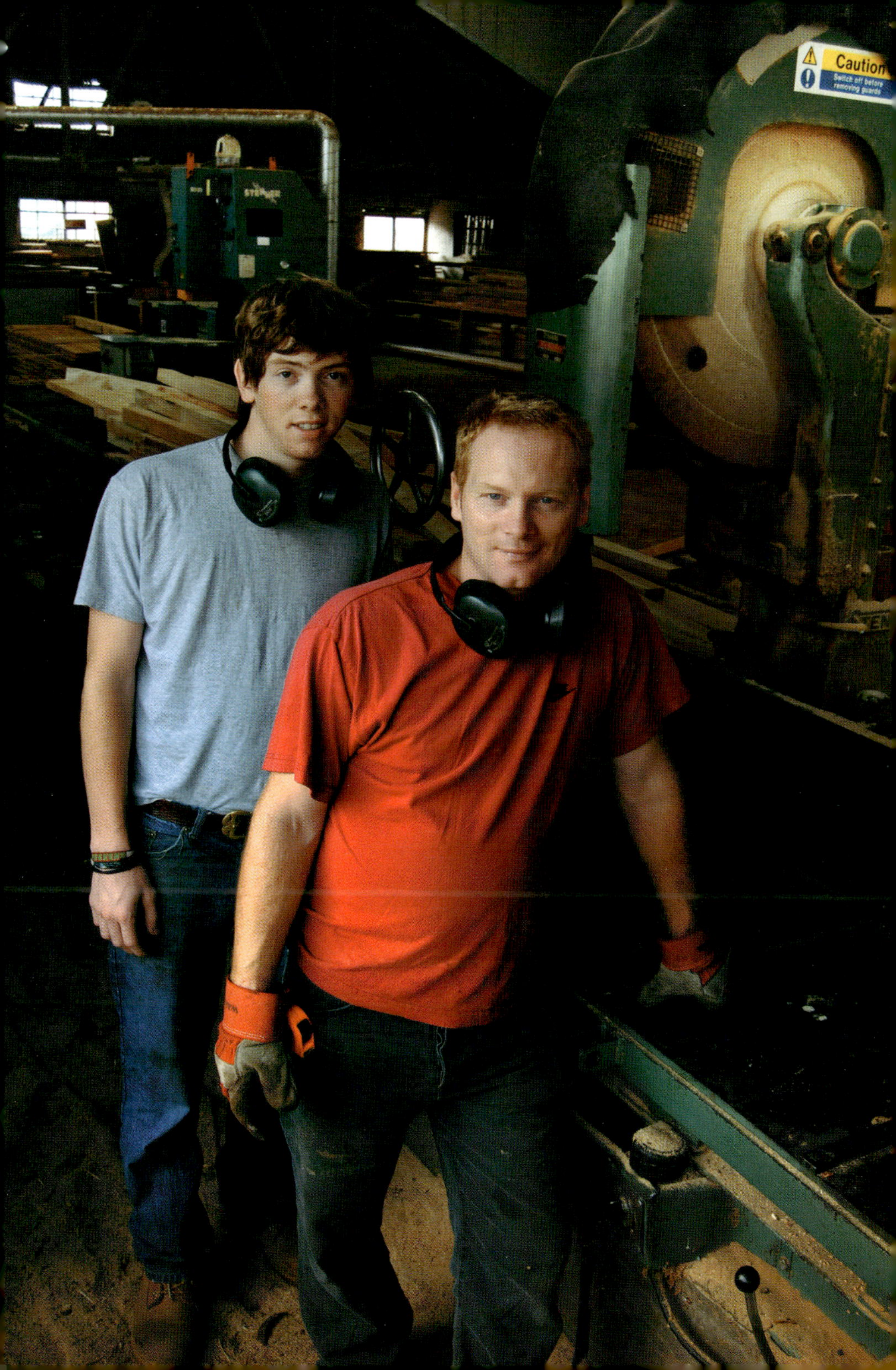
Caution
Switch off before
removing guards

WOODWORKERS

Photographs from the 2002 project (see page 71) to find better uses for oak thinnings. Shown here are Dave Johnson, working on a 'Ten Commandmants' plaque for a South Wales church (opposite); artist and woodworker Tony Randall (below right) in the idiosyncratic doorway of his workshop; and Jim Errington (below) making a lot of sawdust as well an oak corner cupboard.

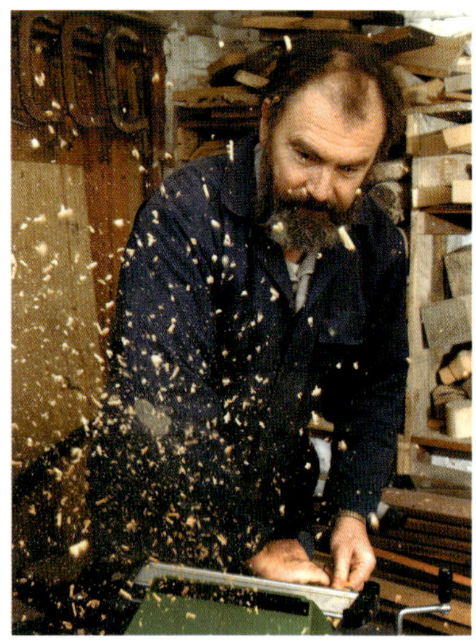

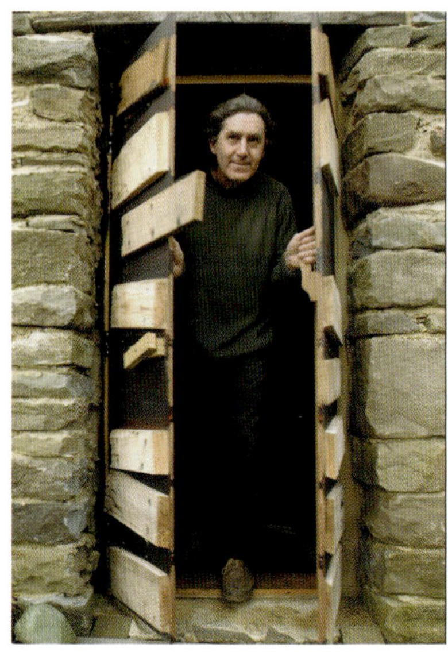

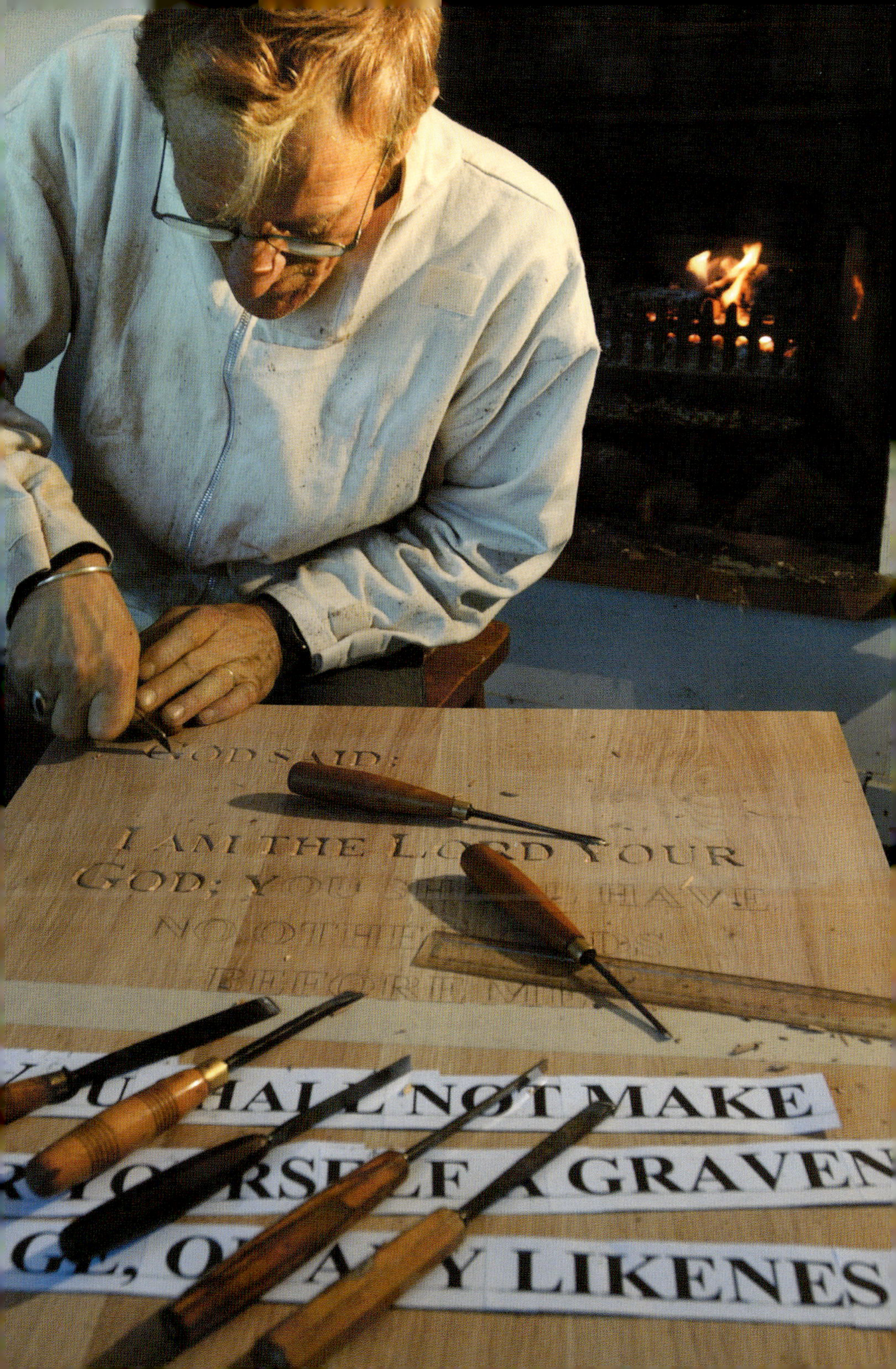

GOD SAID:
I AM THE LORD YOUR
GOD; YOU SHALL HAVE
NO OTHER GODS
BEFORE ME
YOU SHALL NOT MAKE
FOR YOURSELF A GRAVEN
IMAGE, OR ANY LIKENES

Verderers' Court

From the early days of Forest Law, foresters elected four representatives, the Verderers, who met at a building they called Speech House. Today the Verderers sit four times a year in their courtroom at Speech House Hotel (below), passing judgement on matters of grazing, felling and mining. It is the oldest court in the country.

As an ex-officio member of Verderers' Court, Forest Deputy Surveyor Rob Guest has commissioned new chairs for the courtroom. An open competition was won by furniture maker Chris Lewis, seen opposite in his workshop, with a 'maquette' and an unfinished prototype behind him. The chairs form a matching set, but each has individual features. Different woods are used in the decorative tops of the columns, and different Forest materials - stone, coal, iron and bone from a stag's antlers – are inserted into the top of each backrest.

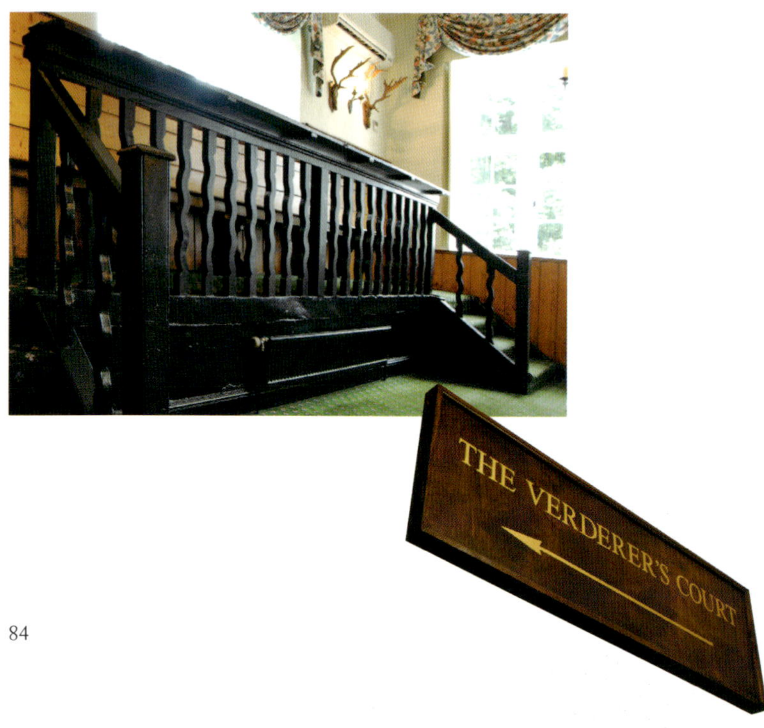

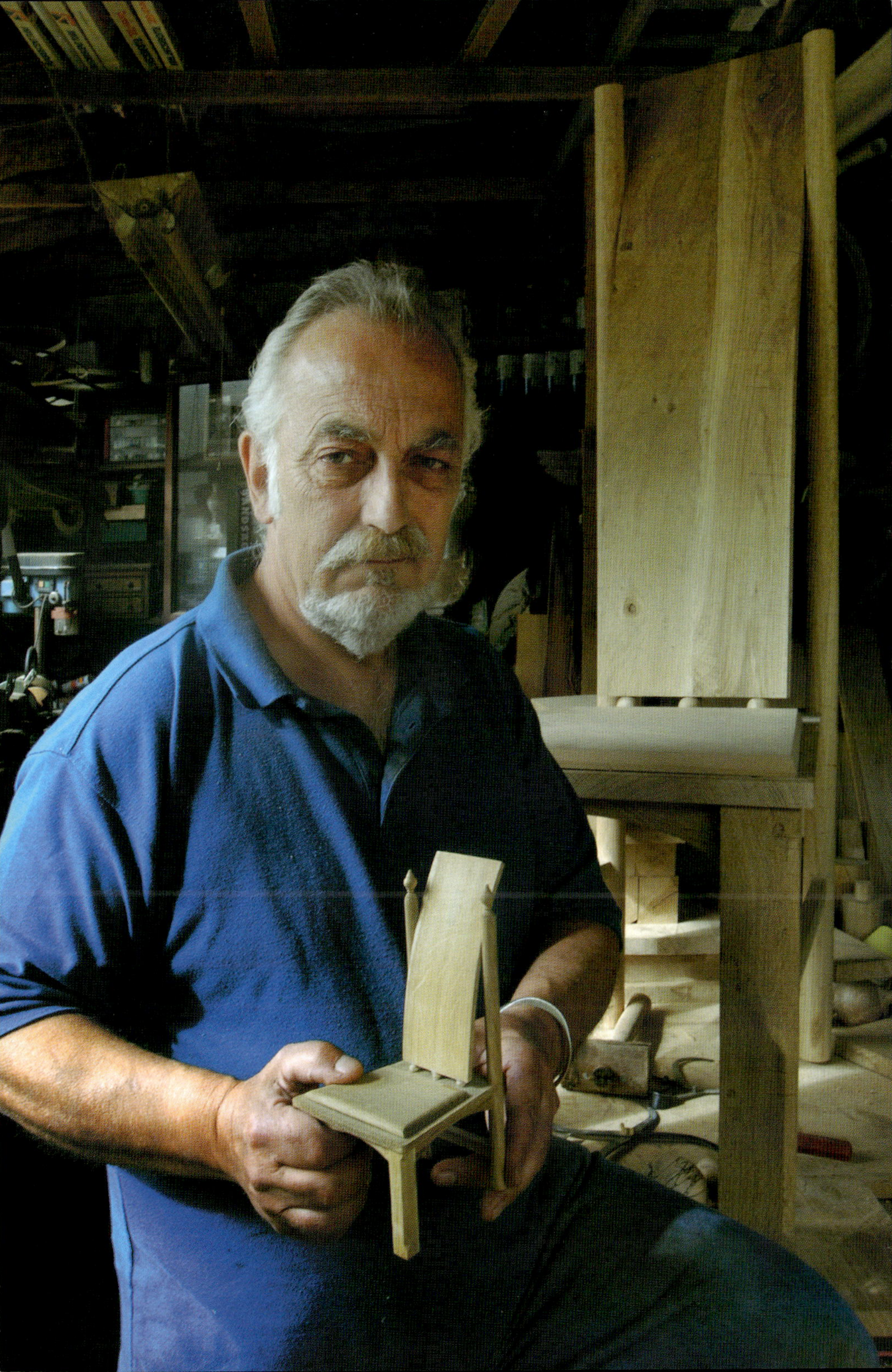

ROB GUEST'S CHOICE

As Deputy Surveyor of the Forest, Rob Guest expects that on retirement his name will be linked to a tree. Pushing aside beech branches, he reveals his choice oak: not a knarled old giant, but a fit 60-year-old, one of a group growing straight and true, close to the 'Observatory' on the Sculpture Trail. En route from Beechenhurst the author was shown another favourite of Rob's, an aspen (below left), one of the tallest in the country.

Below right: As a trustee of the Sculpture Trust, Rob had a hand in commissioning 'Raw' by Neville Gabie, created by felling, cutting and stacking a mature oak in the form of a cube.

Use the Sculpture Trail map available from the Forest visitor centre at Beechenhurst Lodge.

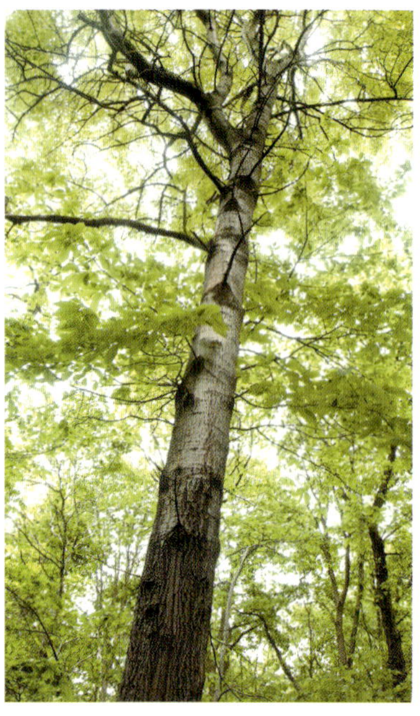

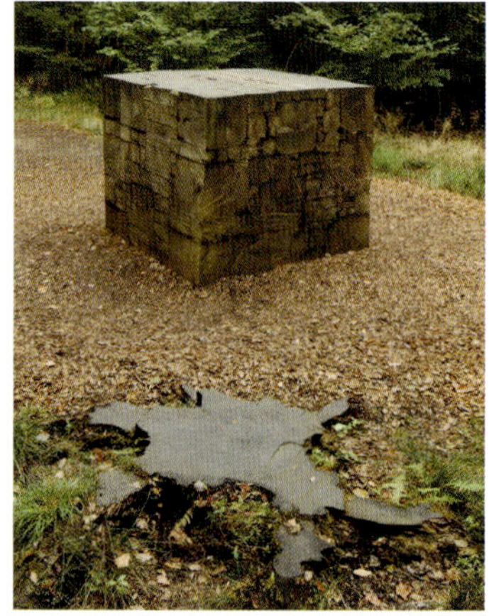

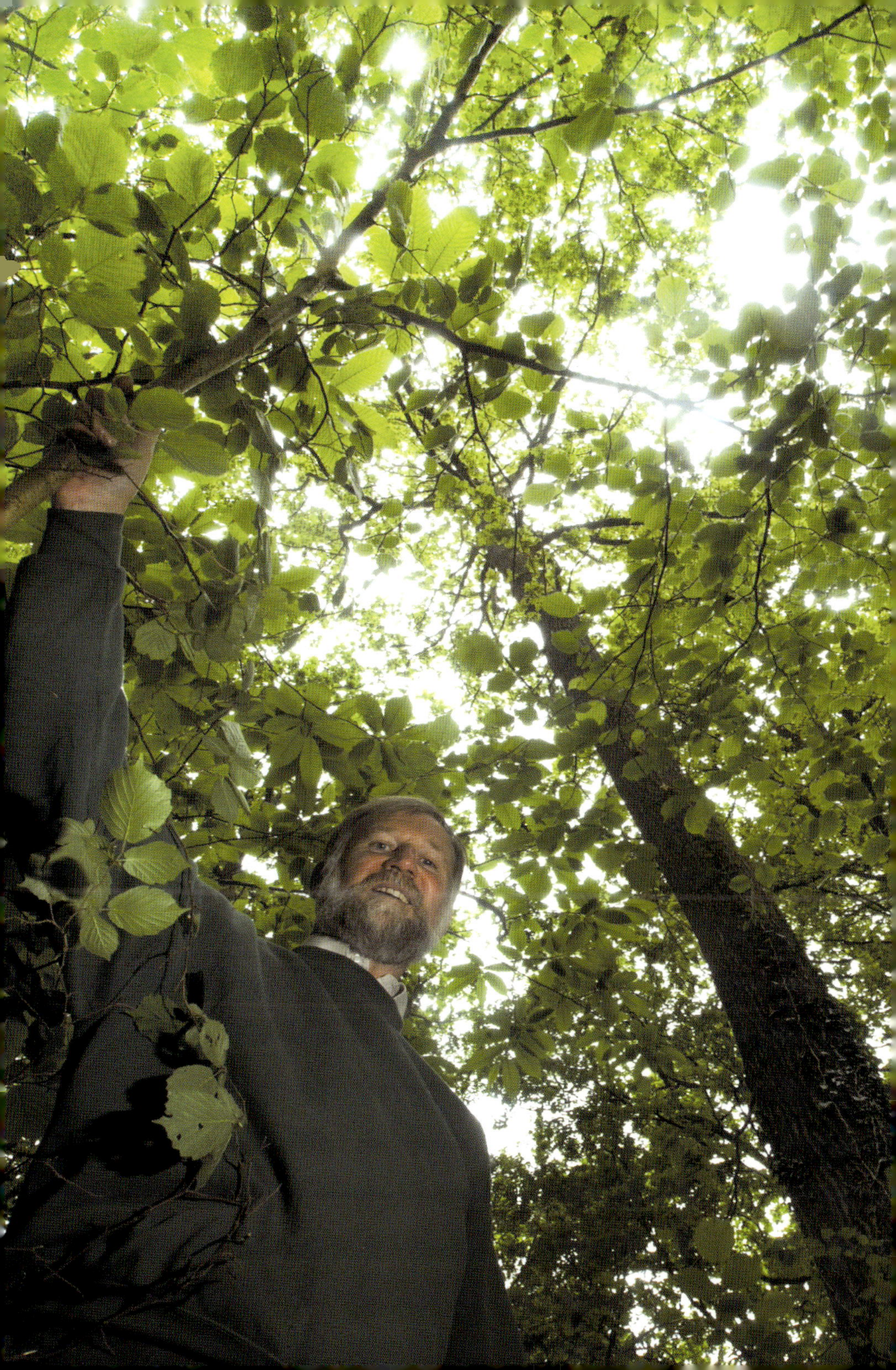

FUN AND GAMES

Orienteers almost always choose wooded cover for their courses, and Dean, with its broken ground from old industrial use, is one of the best areas for the sport in the south of England. The picture below left shows a competitor in the distinctive colours of Harlequins OC hurtling down a silver birch-clad tip at Cannop.

Many of the installations on the Sculpture Trail pay homage to the woods, but 'Melissa's Swing' by Peter Appleton is totally dependent on the sweet chestnut whose branch supports it. Also reliant on the trees is the 'Go Ape' high-wire trail (opposite) which runs though the forest canopy at Mallards Pike.

615122 ('Melissa's Swing'); follow Sculpture Trail map available from the Forest visitor centre at Beechenhurst Lodge. 637092 ('Go Ape')

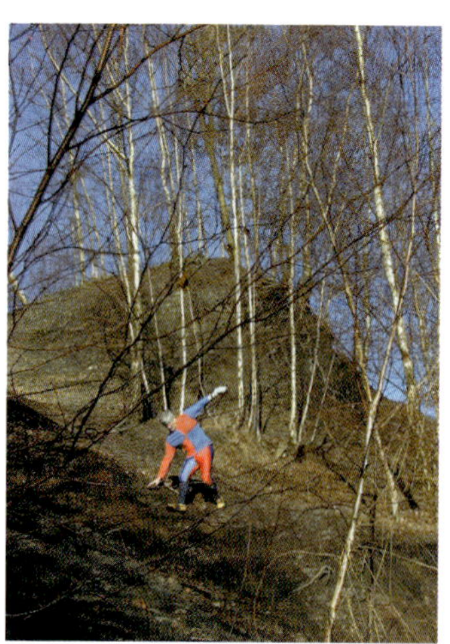

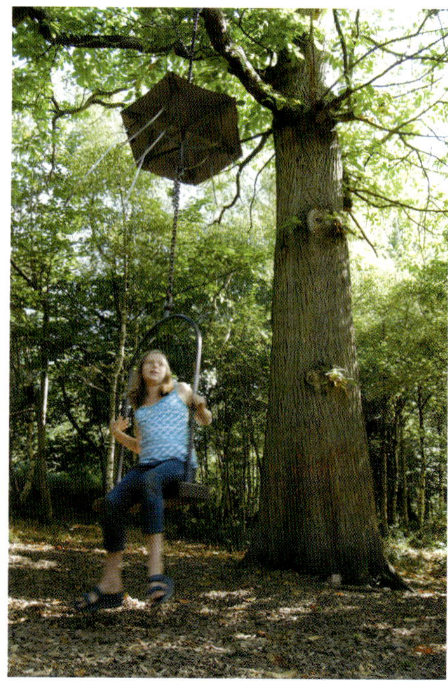

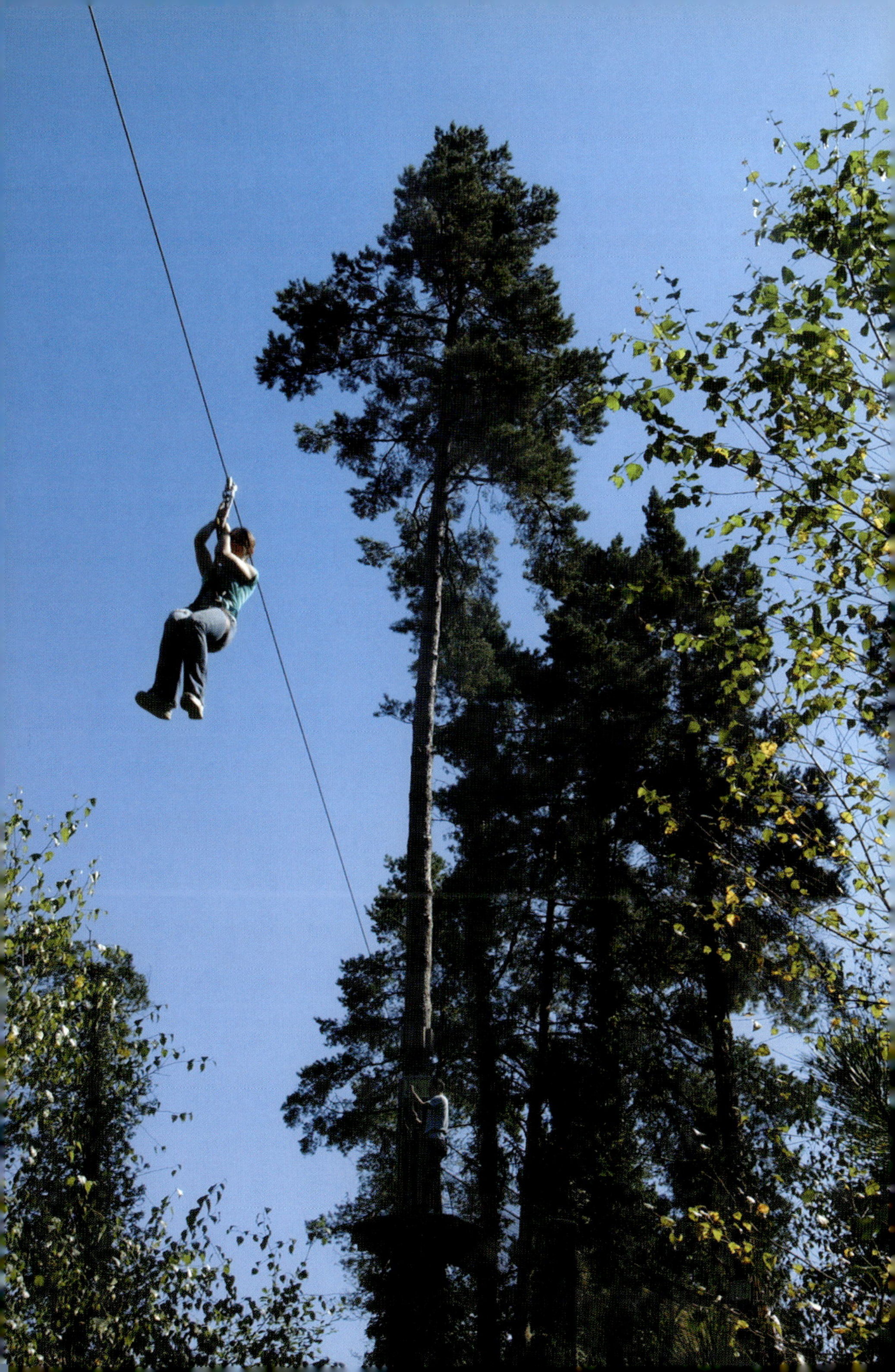

Parkend Primary School

Parkend Primary has made the most of its superb location in the middle of the Forest by forming links with Forest Enterprise via the Arts Council-sponsored Creative Partnership.

During their expedition to measure Charles II oak (see page 12), members of the Year 6 class collected all the different leaves they could find.

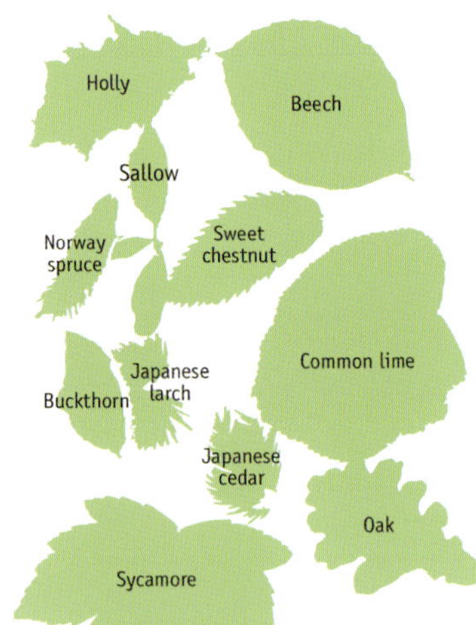

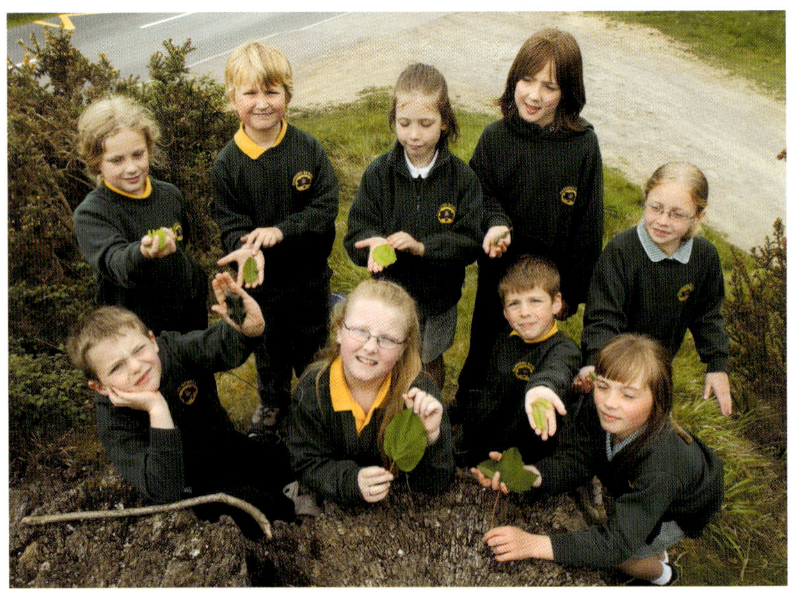

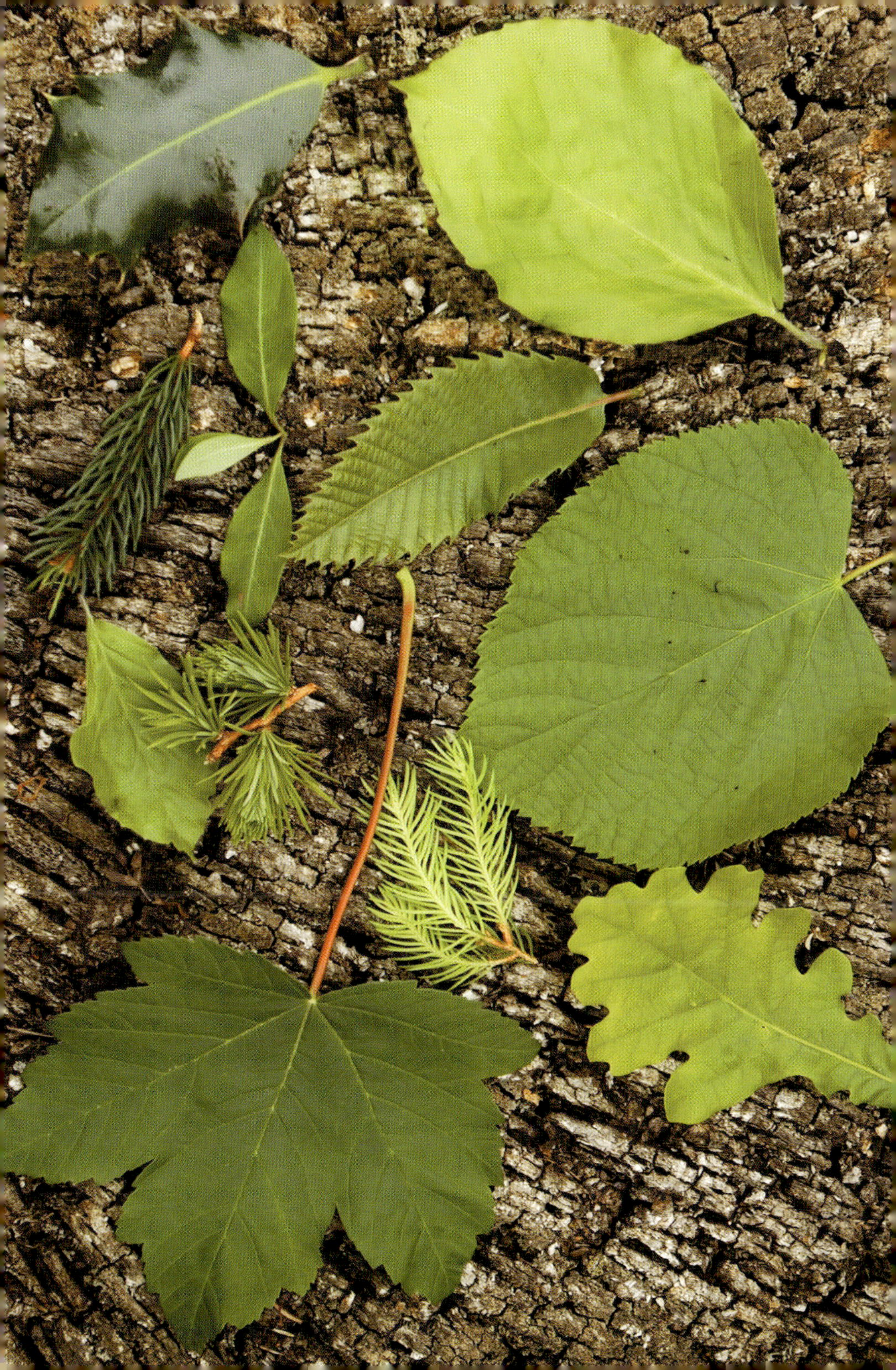

Bream Primary C of E School

The many oaks that punctuate the playground at Bream play a big part in school life. Opposite, Year 3 children show off their paintings for a Year 6 photographic project (part of the school's centenary celebrations for October 2007), while Year 4 children play ring-a-roses (below right).

Below left: During a dry spell, a pupil waters the Trafalgar oak, a sapling planted opposite the school in 2005 to commemorate the bicentenary of the battle of Trafalgar. It stands on the site of an ancient oak known as the 'hard-up-tree' under which out-of-work villagers once queued for employment.

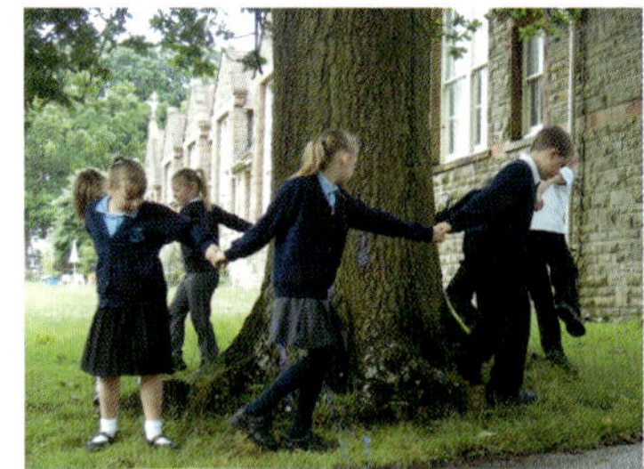

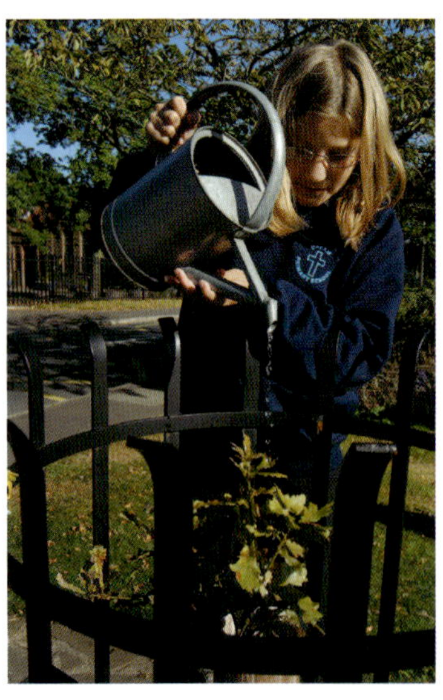

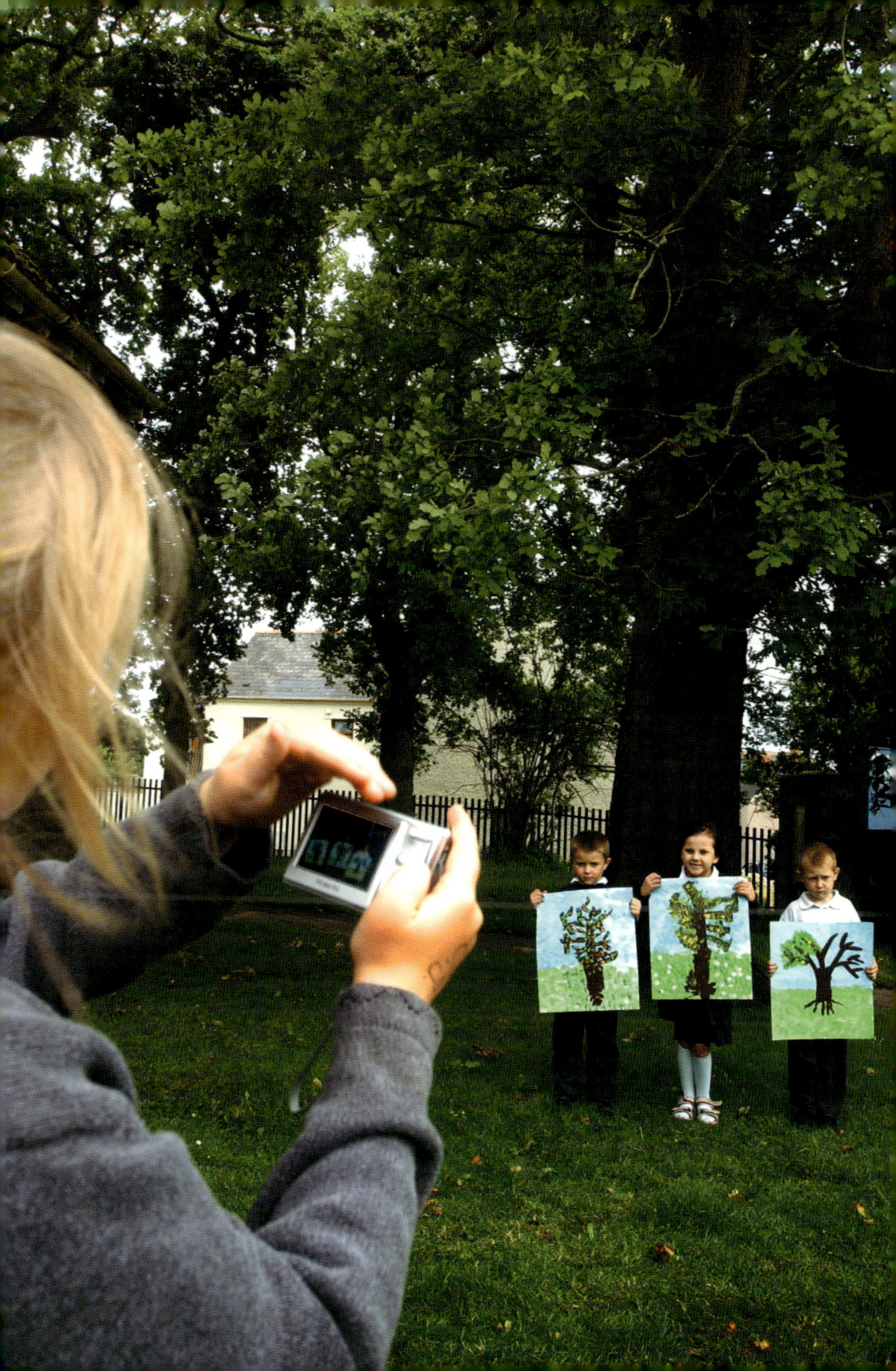

Apples in the Forest

A row of apple trees in blossom leads down to a giant beech, which dominates the driveway at Oaklands Park. The ripe apples and mistletoes are in a Longhope orchard.

Oaklands Park is private but some sections are visible from public paths

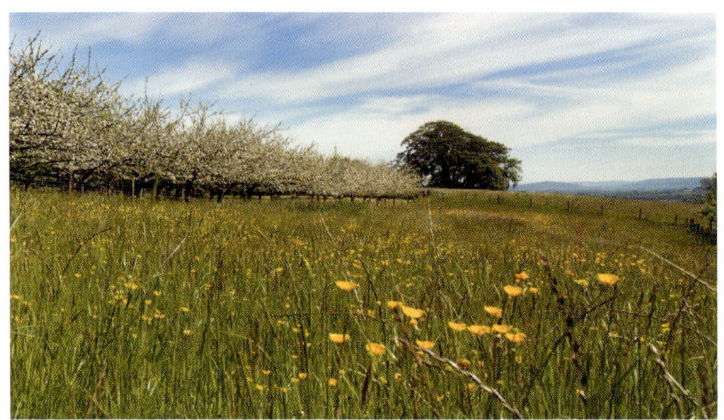

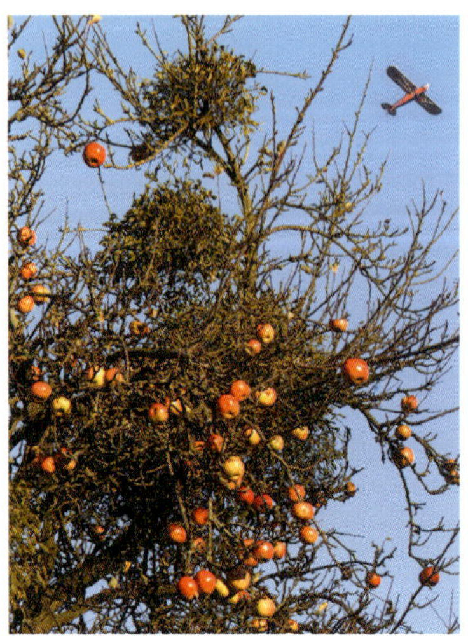

INDEX

ACKNOWLEDGEMENTS

I am grateful for assistance in this project from:

Creative Partnership
Dean Oak Co-operative
Forest Bookshop
Forestry Commission
Lydney Park Estate
Oaklands Park
Sculpture Trust
Parkend Primary School
Bream C of E Primary School

My personal thanks go to Ben Lennon, Nick Assirati, Brian Reece and all those who agreed to appear in this book, especially Ted Merrett for approving the use of the portrait of his late son.

I am indebted to Rob Guest for much advice and for the provision of the foreword, and to my editor and designer Paul Manning.

Many facts are derived from the broadsheet *Interesting Trees in the Forest of Dean* – text by Ian Standing and Fred Savage with additional information by Cyril Hart. More detailed evaluation of Dean's notable trees can be found in Ian Standing's three articles in editions 2, 3 and 4 of the local history society journal *New Regard*.

Both Oaklands and Lydney Park are private estates. They are crossed by public footpaths which run adjacent to some of the trees photographed. Lydney Park opens its parkland and gardens to the public each spring.